FOOD FIGHT

MY PLANT-POWERED JOURNEY
FROM THE BINGO HALLS TO THE BIG TIME

AUSTIN ARIES
WITH MIKE TULLY

PUBLISHED BY GREY BOOKS

Some names and characteristics of individuals have been changed to protect their privacy. Any resulting resemblance to persons living or dead is entirely coincidental and unintentional.

Book design: Tim Harrington

Cover photo / back cover photos: Lee South

Copyright ©2017 Austin Aries with Mike Tully

Print ISBN: 978-0-9982180-0-7

PRINTED IN THE UNITED STATES OF AMERICA

March 2017

First Edition

I'd like to thank all of my fans, friends and family, but most especially my Mom and Dad, Diana, David, Dawn, Justin, Erik and Thea.

DISCLAIMER:

I am not a doctor or a licensed nutritionist.

Hell, if you want to get technical, I might not actually be "The Greatest Man That Ever Lived" either. I'm just a guy who loves vegetables and loves figuring things out for myself.

Which is another way of saying: "This book is written as a source of information only. The information contained in this book is based solely on my personal experience and observations of others and should by no means be considered a substitute for the advice, decision or judgment of the reader's physician or other professional adviser. My publisher and I expressly disclaim responsibility for any adverse effects arising from the use or application of the information contained herein."

Some names and descriptions have been altered to protect the anonymity of individuals.

No animals were harmed in the making of this book.

FOOD FIGHT

MY PLANT-POWERED JOURNEY
FROM THE BINGO HALLS TO THE BIG TIME

INTRODUCTION

When you're a professional wrestler, there are a couple of questions you can count on hearing just about any time you do an interview.

If I talk to people who don't know much about the industry, the first thing they usually want to ask is whether wrestling is fake. For some reason, a lot of people still seem to think there's a 'gotcha' moment to be had by asking about that.

Every wrestler has their own way of answering. I usually point out that my nose has been broken more times than I can remember, and that I didn't just "fake" break it. I remind them that you can't fake gravity. I tell them that the emotion, physicality, and athleticism aren't fake. Oh, and the money I make? That isn't fake, either.

A lot of times people also want to know how or why I got into wrestling. I've developed a bit of a go-to answer for that one, too.

I grew up as an athlete. I made it all the way to college baseball. But I was always kind of a ham, too. I grew up singing in choirs. I took break dancing lessons.

My grandma always used to give me a hard time. "No one likes a show off," she'd say. "Don't toot your own horn." (Based on my career so far, you might have been wrong there, Granny.)

So wrestling is a melting pot of a lot of things I love—athletics and competition, but also theatrics and performance.

After I dropped out of college, I was doing some traveling

and some…not too smart things for cash. Basically, I was young, broke, and trying to figure out my path in life. That's when my childhood best friend called me up out of the blue and told me he was training to be a wrestler.

I wasn't sure how to react at first, but I knew I had to visit him and check it out. When I walked into the garage where he was training and saw the wrestling ring, it blew my mind. I knew this was what I had to do.

A week later, I packed up what little stuff I had, moved onto his couch, started training, and didn't look back. That's basically it.

Growing up, I never really knew what I wanted to be. I just knew I didn't want to be "normal." I had always been looking for a way to live outside the box society tries to put us in and to do things my own way.

And ever since I was a kid, I always loved professional wrestling. So to me, it was fate. I believe the path I'm on is the one I was destined to follow.

Most professional wrestlers answer those two questions all the time, the same as I do. It comes with the territory. For me, though, there's another subject that also comes up a lot.

In 2000, just as I was starting my wrestling career, I gave up eating meat. In 2011, after a gradual evolution, I took what seemed like the next logical step: I cut out all foods containing animal products and switched to a purely plant-based diet.

I didn't make any public announcement. There was no press release. I didn't even fire off a tweet about it. Behind the scenes, I had been teetering on the brink of veganism for some time. To the people close to me, it wasn't really a big deal.

Professionally, though, things were a little different. By then I was pretty well known within the pro wrestling world. And vegetarianism wasn't just part of who I was as a person; it had also become a part of my character. It's something I've mentioned over the years and something announcers have touched on as well. I was known as "The Spectacular Vascular Vegetarian."

So when interviewers brought up the vegetarian angle, I would correct them. Now, I let them know, I was "The Spectacular Vascular Vegan." Slowly but surely, the word spread, especially as I became more visible in the vegan community.

Ever since people in the wrestling world have learned that I am 100% plant-based, at some point or another, pretty much every interview I've done comes around to the same basic set of questions on the subject.

Those usually go something like this:

INTERVIEWER: So…are you really a vegan?

ME: I actually don't like to use that word to describe myself. My wrestling boots are made from leather, and so is the interior of my car.

I prefer to say I eat a plant-based diet or that I'm an herbivore. But yeah, sure, by most people's definition, I'm vegan.

INTERVIEWER: What made you decide to become a vegan?

ME: At the core, I just don't think I ever found eating other creatures very appetizing.

Eating meat is part of how we're raised. Society makes it easy to disconnect yourself from feeling weird about eating meat and encourages you to just do what you're told. So that's what most people do.

As I got older, I began a slow transition. I gave up pork and red meat first to try to eat a little healthier. But then the more I thought about my food, and the more I learned about how it was raised and what it really does to my body, the more uncomfortable I became with consuming any meat at all.

Eventually, after years of educating myself about my food options, I decided I didn't want to eat any animal products—period.

INTERVIEWER: So…does that mean you live on lettuce and

carrots?

ME: Yeah, and I poop little pellets and Cadbury Eggs, too.

Seriously though, there are tons of delicious plant-based foods. As a matter of fact, I've been able to find plant-based versions of all the things I used to enjoy as a meat eater, and they satisfy my cravings just fine. To tell you the truth, I probably have more variety in my diet than the average meat eater does.

INTERVIEWER: But you're a pro wrestler. How do you get enough protein?

ME: The same way everybody does: By eating food!

It's not nearly as hard as people think. Protein comes from all sorts of food sources. In terms of percentage of protein to overall calories, many vegetable and veggie-based foods have just as much if not more protein than meat.

INTERVIEWER: Fine. But isn't that kind of diet ridiculously expensive?

ME: It can be. But cancer is pretty expensive, too. And from what I gather, that's what people get when they live on a steady diet of meat and animal products and a bunch of other things that the FDA, in its infinite wisdom, has approved for all of us to eat. I don't think most people are aware of the true health consequences of the all-American diet.

Look, any diet can be expensive. But when it comes to buying food, prioritizing convenience costs way more than prioritizing health.

One of the most expensive things you can do is to eat out a lot. And some people eat out for every single meal. Why don't interviewers ever ask people why they spend so much money on pre-packaged, processed, convenient shit?

INTERVIEWER: You travel all the time. It must be difficult getting food on the road.

ME: It can be. Preparation is the key. But that doesn't just apply to me. That goes for anybody who works away from home and doesn't want to stuff their face with fast food all day and night.

INTERVIEWER: *So...no meat? At all?*

ME: No. I don't eat anything with a face. Except my lady.

INTERVIEWER: *But...don't you miss bacon?*

ME: Nope. You can buy great variations of plant-based bacons. Bacon's actually a really distinct flavor that's pretty easily replicated with liquid smoke and maple syrup and stuff like that. I make awesome BLTs all the time. Except mine aren't loaded with saturated fat and cholesterol.

And I definitely don't miss the part where a bunch of animals had to be mistreated and then die just so I could eat a sandwich.

INTERVIEWER: *Isn't it weird to know you'll never eat cheese again?*

ME: "Weird" is a relative term. To be honest, I think it's weird that human beings consume another species' milk at all, especially after we're fully grown. We're the only creatures on earth who do that.

A mother cow makes milk to feed to her baby. But instead, we take her baby, steal her milk, mechanically re-impregnate her, make cheese out of the stolen milk, and then eat it ourselves. Rinse and repeat.

Admit it—if you say it out loud, doesn't that sound a little weird to you, too?

INTERVIEWER: *Oh...so you think I'm a dick because I eat cheese and meat?*

ME: No, I don't look down on people because they choose to eat meat or animal products. For the first 20-plus years of my life, I ate meat and I don't think I was a dick. (Well, some people would say I was a dick. But that's not meat's fault.)

I just think that if people did some homework and learned some of the stuff I've learned, they might make some different decisions about the way they eat. That's all.

Over the last couple of years, I don't know how many times I've had that conversation. One of the initial reasons I wrote this book was just to get all those answers down in one place. Who knows? Maybe the next person who interviews me will read this, and then I won't have to run through all those same questions all over again.

But more importantly, I wanted to write a book because, based on my experiences talking about a plant-based diet both publicly and with family and friends, I've seen just how many people are interested in the subject. For every commenter on Instagram who says, "Why don't you just eat a steak and shut up, asshole?" there's someone else who hits me up because they genuinely want to learn more.

I've encountered a lot of curiosity about the plant-based foods I eat and about diet in general. I've also found that when it comes to vegetarianism, veganism, and just making informed decisions about food, there's an awful lot of ignorance out there.

I don't necessarily blame people. For a long time, I was completely in the dark about all this stuff, too. Things are getting better, but there are still people who don't really know the difference between a vegetarian and a vegan.

Believe me—I've had some unbelievable conversations over the years.

"So, do vegetarians still eat fish? Because fish aren't really animals, right?"

Someone seriously asked me that a few years back.

"No," I replied. "Believe it or not, fish technically qualify as animals."

"Sure," he said. "But it's not *really* an animal. It's a fish."

"Have you ever been to the zoo?" I asked him.

"Yes."

"And what do they have at the zoo?"

"Animals."

"Did you see any fish at the zoo?"

"Yes."

"Hmm. So a fish is a fucking animal."

Once again: That conversation actually happened one time.

Based on what I've seen, I believe that many people are genuinely open to change. Some people just haven't been exposed to all the facts. But if they were, they might look at things differently and make different decisions.

If you think you might be one of those people, then this book is for you.

And if you *don't* think you're one of those people, then hopefully this book is *really* for you.

Throughout my life, I've met tons of people and had tons of experiences that have planted little seeds of thought in my head. I may not have realized they were happening at the time—or, in some cases, until years later—but some of those seeds eventually sprouted in my mind and helped lead me down my current path.

If you're curious at all about why I have chosen the diet I have, I hope that maybe this book can plant a little seed in *your* mind.

As I tell you my story, I'll try avoid to getting too preachy or sounding too negative. I'm not trying to climb up on some sanctimonious soapbox here. I don't want to be the guy who just tries to make everybody feel shitty about killing a bunch of animals.

Sure, I've heard lots of obnoxious, ill-informed commentary about my diet from people who eat meat. But truthfully, I see some pretty obnoxious stuff coming out of the plant-based community, too. Vegans and vegan organizations are sometimes guilty of talking down to everybody who doesn't already agree with them. I'm not interested in doing that.

I spent a lot of time eating meat, and by now I've spent a lot of time eating a plant-based diet. I'd like to think I understand where both sides are coming from. So as I see it, my job here is to be an ambassador and to try and bridge the gap between the two camps. It's easy to forget that eating meat or being plant-based doesn't have to be an all-or-nothing decision.

Let me explain. I know some people would consider a plant-based diet like mine a little extreme. And from the point of view most of us were raised with, it is. Consuming absolutely no animal products, ever, is obviously not the norm.

But here's a question to consider: When's the last time you sat down and had a meal that contained zero animal products? I'm not talking about a snack, like an apple or something. I mean a full meal with no meat, no dairy, and no eggs.

Maybe you recently had some pasta with marinara sauce? Fine, but did you read the label? Even if you didn't sprinkle Parmesan on top, there was probably some cheese or some butter in the sauce to begin with.

You almost have to go out of your way to eat a truly vegan meal, especially at a restaurant, where there's bound to be a little butter or animal broth involved in just about every product they serve.

When you break it down, if you're like a lot of people I talk to, you might have a hard time remembering your last completely animal-free meal. And if you ask me, eating animals or animal-derived products at every single meal is *also* pretty extreme.

In this book, I'm not going to ask anyone to jump from their extreme to my extreme. I'm under no illusion that anyone reading this right now is going to immediately swear off animal products forever, join PETA, and go buy a "Tofu Nation" T-shirt. We all know that isn't going to happen. (And for reasons I'll explain later, if you tried to go vegan overnight, chances are it wouldn't even stick.)

I'd just like to show you that there are a wide spectrum of

dietary options available to choose from. And I'd like to ask you to think about where you sit on that spectrum, and then to maybe consider taking a few steps closer to the middle. That's all.

The last—and maybe most important—reason I decided to write a book is because I find that when people ask about my diet, they tend to miss the point. They always focus on veganism. I understand why that is, but to me, there's always been way more to the conversation than "to meat or not to meat."

I do believe the world would be a better, healthier, and happier place if more people chose a plant-based lifestyle. But ultimately, my diet isn't really about veganism. It's about exercising my right to make informed choices about the food I eat, vegan or not.

It's about being aware of how the food that's being marketed at me is grown (or made in a lab, as the case may be). It's about what additives or preservatives or chemicals might have been added on the way from farm to table. Ultimately, it's about taking control back from the corporate food industry that has embedded itself in all of our lives and that tries to dictate what we eat, regardless of the consequences their products have for our health and for our planet.

I'm deeply passionate about the food I choose to eat. I believe that being educated about food is a vital part of living to your full potential. And I am blown away by how little attention our society pays to the subject.

As far as I can tell, most people never make time to take a good hard look at the things they choose to put in their mouths. Our entire culture is set up to make you think that as long as you don't live on McDonald's, and you eat your veggies, and you occasionally choose supermarket labels that say "fat-free" or "all-natural," then you're on the right track.

As a result, many people don't know the nutritional realities of so many of the terrible foods we eat—both animal *and* plant-based—all with our government's explicit approval. Until I started my journey, I personally had no idea.

Even if people decide to do some homework about the food they eat, the answers aren't always easy to find if you don't know where to look. That's where this book comes in.

If more people were equipped with the right information, I believe a lot of them would open their eyes and become more mindful of their place on this planet and what kind of system they do—or do not—want to contribute to.

Really, it just starts with giving a fuck.

There might not be anything I can say or do to make some people reevaluate the way they look at food. Certain people are set in their ways and their lifestyle and the food that they eat. No amount of sad footage of animals being slaughtered is going to change their mind. And neither will all the research which has demonstrated the relationship between cancer and a high intake of dairy and meat, not to mention the health risks associated with many (if not most) of the products that line the shelves of our local supermarkets. Some people just flat out don't give a shit.

But I think most of us can agree that eating a little more fresh, healthy, plant-based food and cutting back on the frozen processed meat lover's pizzas is probably better for our overall well-being. I think there are probably a couple of other things most of us can agree on, too, like how eating more plants and less animals is better for the planet, and how cutting back on eating animals and animal products could probably eliminate a lot of animal cruelty, too.

Maybe you're like me. Maybe you also want to skip the easy route that society has laid out for you. Maybe it's also important to you to look beneath the surface of things, make your own decisions, and forge your own path.

Maybe that pertains to the food you eat. Maybe it just pertains to life in general.

But either way, if that's the case, then hopefully there's something about my journey that can help you make your way through your own.

CHAPTER 1

Wisconsin might well be the most meat-eating, dairy-loving place on earth.

You could probably say the same thing about the whole Midwest, or really about America in general. But Wisconsin—the place where I grew up—takes it to a whole different level. The entire culture seems to revolve around beer and bratwursts and cheese and sports and hunting and fishing.

Look at it this way: There are three pro sports teams in Wisconsin—the Green Bay Packers, the Milwaukee Brewers, and the Milwaukee Bucks.

Packers fans, as you probably know, are called "Cheese-heads." They literally wear huge foam cheese hats. And by the way, the cheese-themed accessories aren't limited to hats. There are cheese-shaped beer holders. There are cheese ties. There are cheese tiaras. You get the picture. People in Wisconsin actually buy and wear all that stuff.

Meanwhile, the highlight of every Brewers home game is not the $6 beers or the "Brat-chos," but when a bunch of guys dressed up as sausages race each other around the diamond with the crowd cheering on their favorite.

And then there are the Bucks, who are named after the animals that many in Wisconsin enjoy going out to kill, and then sticking on top of their cars.

I grew up in Waukesha, a suburb west of Milwaukee, in what I would call a typical lower-middle class Midwestern family. My parents married young, and shortly after that they had me. I became the oldest of four kids—two boys and two girls.

We lived in a modest house. Old station wagons and Ford Tempos frequently occupied the driveway. Our wardrobe was mainly made up of generous hand-me-downs and the finest clothes Goodwill had to offer. For better or worse, the barbershop we went to was called "Super Moms Cuts." And let me tell you, some of those cuts were just *super.*

Money was always tight for my family. My parents pinched pennies and cut corners. Sometimes they robbed Peter to pay Paul. But we lived a basically normal life, and we had everything we needed.

My dad busted his ass to make sure we always had a roof over our head. We might have bought the generic cereal at the supermarket and drank the generic soda, but there was always enough to eat.

Mom did what she could to make sure the money got stretched as far as it could go. If we had spaghetti for dinner, she would always do that trick where you fill the empty container of meat sauce back up halfway with water and then dump that out into the pot, to really get the most out of the jar. It was a family of six trying to stretch a dollar to make sure everybody got fed.

I wouldn't say cooking was my mom's specialty. She wasn't awful, but it wasn't something she enjoyed, either. It was really just another job she had on top of all the other things she had to worry about. In addition to raising four kids of her own, she also worked a job at a daycare center to bring home extra money.

Mom was part of the generation where the microwave became a staple in every kitchen. The old world of June Cleaver spending all day whipping up a homemade chicken pot pie was replaced by moms like mine nuking a frozen, pre-packaged, some-kinda-meat pot pie for 15 minutes.

Cooking food from scratch used to be more of a necessity back in the old days. But by the time I was a kid, fast food, frozen pizzas, microwaveable entrées, and all that kind of stuff were taking over. Ready-to-eat foods made it easy—and cheap—for overworked parents on a tight budget to put food on the table.

Now compared to my father, my mom was an Iron Chef. My dad sometimes worked two jobs, so he wasn't pitching in a whole lot in the kitchen anyway. But if my mom ever got sick, or if dad had to cook for some reason, he was famous for grabbing whatever he found in the fridge and whatever vegetables he had grown in the garden and then throwing all that stuff in a pot. And that was dinner.

By the time the food was ready, you weren't always sure what the original ingredients might have been, but when it was dad's turn to cook, there wasn't a whole lot of negotiating at the dinner table. You knew to just shut up and dig in to dad's "stew."

Food-wise, I'd say it was a typical all-American upbringing for that time. On a weeknight, a family dinner might have been a couple of Jack's frozen pizzas and an iceberg lettuce salad with ranch, or maybe some boxed mac and cheese with hot dogs, or some burgers. Stuff like that.

Looking back, I'd say one of my all-time favorite foods as a kid was KFC. On the rare occasion that my family would go eat out, I loved getting some fried chicken and then washing that down with some Mountain Dew. In my world, that was a tasty score back then.

Another memorable treat was eating hot cakes and sausage at McDonald's. My Grandma Ginny and Grandpa Gerd, from my mom's side, lived three blocks from a McDonald's. In summertime, we'd always stop there for breakfast on our way over to go swimming.

Grandpa Gerd was a lieutenant in the armed forces. He jumped out of airplanes at night during World War II. As a kid, that sounded pretty crazy to me. It still does now, come to think of it.

After raising four kids, Grandma Ginny went to work as a waitress at a place called Zorba's. She'd bring me rice pudding from work all the time. Rice, sugar, milk, sugar, raisins, sugar, and cinnamon. As a kid, how can you go wrong with that?

Other times, we'd be driving down the street with Grandpa Gerd and he'd make an abrupt right turn at Tallenger's, a little local soft-serve ice cream place.

"What's the naughty car doing?" he would ask as he argued with the car, pretending he couldn't control the steering wheel. That was one of grandpa's classic gags.

And then he'd pull in and we'd all get vanilla-chocolate swirl ice cream cones.

When it came to the stuff we ate, we were more or less like everyone else in the neighborhood. I imagine many people reading this can relate in one way or another. The word "organic" did not come up in our house. There were no debates about GMO versus non-GMO, or the dangers of saturated fats.

For at least the first 20 years of my life, I don't recall ever meeting anyone who identified as a vegetarian, much less as a vegan. If I did, obviously they didn't make a very strong impression on me, because I don't remember them.

My dad used to put too much salt on his food, which is probably what gave him high blood pressure later on. But, in our world, no one looked at that as a failure on his part, or thought he ate irresponsibly.

High blood pressure was a common problem. People just accepted that some people got high blood pressure. It was kind of like it wasn't your fault if your diet was dangerously high in sodium. People treated salt as if it was completely unavoidable—as if food somehow came off the farm that way.

It's kind of like the way people used to look at cigarettes. When I was growing up, both of my parents smoked. That wasn't unusual among my friends' parents, either. That's the way things were. As far as I can recall, no one really questioned it.

14

That's the world I grew up in. That's where my story starts. Where I come from, no one took a really hard look at the food we were eating or asked if there might be a better way. People just accepted what they were given and ate the foods they were told they should eat.

That's the way people were in general where I grew up. Everyone tended to fall in line. No one really questioned what you're supposed to do with your life, either.

Other than wrestling, I can only ever remember having one career plan in mind. Way back when I was three years old or so, I got it in my head that when I grew up I might join the military. Grandpa Gerd was in WWII, my other grandfather had fought in the Korean War, and both my uncles on my mom's side went to Vietnam. So I thought I might follow in their footsteps someday.

I think becoming a soldier seemed like an attainable goal, since so many of my family members had gone down that path. That seemed like a trajectory I might already be on at that young age.

I had this yearbook with my uncles' Army pictures in it from back when they were in boot camp. I also had some old practice bullets and my grandpa's old practice grenade. G.I. Joe was big at the time, so I had all those toys, too. I used to take all my Army stuff in the backyard with me and camp out in a tent. My grandfather gave me the old trunk that had sat at the foot of his bed when he was in the service, and I dragged that into my room and kept all my Army stuff inside it. Playing with Army stuff was my big thing for probably about two years.

But then one Saturday morning, everything changed, the first time I saw AWA wrestling on TV.

Wrestling grabbed me instantly. The first AWA matches I ever saw must have been all the way back in '82 or '83. I remember watching Blackjack Lanza and Bobby Heenan versus Hulk Hogan in a cage, back when Hulk was still in the AWA, a year or so before Hulkamania exploded.

(And yes, I do mean *that* Bobby Heenan. People probably remember him more as Bobby "The Brain" from a few years later. But not only was Bobby Heenan a great manager and commentator, he was tremendous in the ring, too.)

Wrestling became one of the things I had in common with my dad. I remember going down to the Mecca Arena as a kid and reaching over the guardrail and patting Jesse Ventura on the ass as he walked down the aisle on his way to the ring. My dad gave me a stern look for that one.

"Don't ever reach over the guardrail," he said. "If you touch the wrestlers, they can touch you back, and there's nothing I can do about that."

That's when I learned that you don't ever put your hands on a wrestler.

I also discovered the NWA. There were the Four Horsemen: Ric Flair, Arn Anderson, Ole Anderson, and Tully Blanchard. Then they kicked Ole out and brought in Barry Windham and then Lex Luger...and then, much later, Steve "Mongo" McMichael (although I've since tried to forget about that).

And then there were the Road Warriors. To this day, I can't hear "Iron Man" by Black Sabbath and not picture those two beasts hitting the ring and beating the hell out of a couple of poor souls.

Out of Texas, there was World Class Championship Wrestling with the Von Erichs and the Freebirds, before this crazy guy named Cactus Jack showed up.

The WWE—then the WWF—was around then, too. I watched, of course. To me, it had a different feel, though. It was a little more over-the-top. You had Hulk Hogan saying prayers and eating vitamins. There was "Rowdy" Roddy Piper and his Hot Rod shirt and kilt. And then there was "The Barber," always trying to cut everybody's hair off.

And for some weird reason, there were always a lot of animals involved. "Birdman" Koko B. Ware had his parrot, Frankie. There were the British Bulldogs with their bulldog, Matilda, and then Jake "The Snake" Roberts had his python, Damien.

From the start, while I enjoyed the glitz and glamor of sports entertainment, I really gravitated to the dark and dingy presentation of rasslin.' That's what initially grabbed my imagination.

I also gravitated toward the smaller, more athletic guys, and the underdogs. Everyone loves Hulk Hogan, but deep down inside, most of us know we'll never be him. It doesn't matter how much heart you have; most people are just never going to be 6'6" and 300 pounds. But when they look at guys like Ricky Morton, the 1-2-3 Kid (later known as X-Pac), or even an Austin Aries, I think they can identify with that on a more personal level.

As a kid, I remember rooting for a guy named Jake "The Milkman" Milliman. He never won his matches but ended up getting a little cult following because of how well he played the underdog role. And then there were the Mulkey Brothers, who took an ass kicking so good that people started to get behind them. And after Jim Cornette mockingly coined the term "Mulkey Mania," they lucked their way into their first ever victory and people went nuts!

Once I discovered wrestling, it quickly became an all-consuming passion for me. It was also a pretty good physical outlet for a very active little dude. I used to practice throwing dropkicks against an inner tube in my grandma's pool. My aunt (who's also my godmother) made me a big, boxy, fuzzy horse out of foam. The thing was three feet tall, and I practiced my moves on that thing all the time until I finally trashed it a couple years later.

As soon as the wrestling bug bit me, I started begging my parents for wrestling figures to play with. The first WWF action figures were those old rubber ones that were frozen in one pose. You couldn't really do shit with those toys.

But then, around 1985, Remco came out with toys that were a lot closer to the action figures you see today. The arms and legs moved, which made them a lot more fun to play with. On my eighth birthday, my mom made me a birthday cake that looked like a wrestling ring, and there were Rick Martel and Baron von Raschke toys on top of the cake. Pretty much from then on, I was obsessed with getting my hands on as many wrestling figures as humanly possible.

My mom used to take me down to Kmart and put all the wrestling toys I wanted on layaway. Yes, layaway. A lot of people reading this probably don't even know what layaway means, since nowadays everyone has a credit card. But when I was a kid, that was how we bought a lot of stuff. Mom would make a down payment, and Kmart would hold the toys off the shelves and then give them to her once she finished paying for them.

Whenever new figures came out, my mom would grab them all for me and put them on layaway so they wouldn't sell out before she could afford to pay for them. Once they were paid off, she would take them home and hide all of them up in her bedroom closet.

That was a brilliant strategy on her part, because it gave her a lot of leverage with me. Mom knew that I knew that she had the toys, and she knew I was desperate to get my hands on them. Whenever I did a bunch of chores, or something else that was worthy of a little reward, she would take all the new toys out of her closet and let me pick which ones I wanted to open up.

I used to spend hours thinking about those action figures. Which one would I open next? On one hand, I could get the Midnight Riders. But I also really wanted that Carlos Colón and Abdullah the Butcher combination pack. Then again, if I got the Nick Bockwinkel and Ric Flair combo, I could make them a tag team, but I could also pit them against each other as rivals. When you're a little kid, these are critical decisions we're talking about.

Eventually, I created this massive collection. I'd say I had 50 or 60 of those things. I used to wrestle my guys against each other on top of my grandpa's old military trunk. One Christmas, I got the toy WWF ring. My mom had wrapped everything separately. I opened the ropes and the turnbuckles first and couldn't figure out what the hell it was. When I unwrapped the actual ring and realized what I had on my hands I started freaking out. But the funny thing was, after the novelty wore off, that ring couldn't compare to my Grandpa's trunk.

As the wrestling toys started piling up, slowly but surely the military stuff all got packed away—for good. Except that Army trunk, now filled with wrestlers, of course.

Although I didn't realize it at the time, I think I always had an interest in the business done behind the curtain in wrestling. When I had played with my Army stuff, I always pretended I was a soldier. But when I played wrestling, I never played as a wrestler. I always played as the guy controlling the wrestlers.

I started my own imaginary promotion. There was already the WWF and the NWA and the AWA and WCCW. So I called my promotion the CWA—The Classic Wrestling Association. I split all my toys up into good guys and bad guys and tag teams.

When my mom went shopping at Kmart, I would sit in the magazine section and read all the wrestling mags—*The Wrestler, Inside Wrestling, Pro Wrestling Illustrated*. The magazines had all the rankings of the major promotions, but then they'd also have a side column with all the smaller promotions. And in my head, I would pluck guys from the small promotions to come wrestle for the CWA.

I went to some pretty extreme lengths at times. If necessary, I would change an action figure's name and his gimmick and turn him into a whole new wrestler. If I had a Ric Flair figure, for example, I couldn't just keep him as Ric Flair, because everyone knew the "Nature Boy" wrestled in the NWA.

So I would get some paint and then color his hair and give him a moustache. Or I would turn his short tights into long tights, or maybe give him some face paint. My grandma was into sewing and she always had material lying around, so sometimes I would give my guys a whole new wardrobe.

And I wasn't just limited to using my wrestler toys. The Remco-style wrestling toys weren't just more flexible and user-friendly than the old WWF figurines, they were also smaller—about five or six inches tall—which made them the same size as a bunch of other toys. And remember, this was a golden age of action figures. In addition to wrestlers and G.I. Joes, there was also He-Man and the ThunderCats. Stallone had some Rambo and Rocky figures. There were some Schwarzenegger ones, too. Hell, Chuck Norris even got in on the action. And then, of course, stores like Walgreens had generic rip-off versions of all the big toys.

Since these toys were all about the same size, I soon found out that certain heads and arms and legs were interchangeable with one another. Very quickly, the CWA had a wide variety of performers to choose from.

I turned Lion-O from the ThunderCats into a guy called "Big Red." The ThunderCats toys were a little bigger than the other action figures, so Big Red was a "Mean" Mark Callous (AKA The Undertaker) kind of guy, with a great clothesline and a big boot to stick in his opponent's face.

I remember I had one guy I called "The Zodiac Warrior" and another one called "The Black Ninja." Not necessarily the most original nicknames ever conceived. But then again, in my defense, I was pretty young.

Other than thinking about joining the military, way back when I was basically a toddler, I don't think I've ever wanted to do anything with my life but wrestle. So I would love to tell you that, ever since I was five years old, I was 100% committed to becoming a professional wrestler. But it wasn't until many years later that I set my mind to pursuing that dream.

When I was a kid, I don't think it ever dawned on me that I could actually become a wrestler myself and be up there in the ring like those guys I saw on TV and down at the Mecca. Sure, I loved watching wrestling and playing with my toys. But even if

I had decided I wanted to wrestle, and my parents had somehow been on board, how would I have even gotten started?

If you want to be a rock star, as far-fetched as that might sound, you can at least go get some guitar lessons and get the ball rolling a little bit. But pro wrestling isn't going to be a varsity sport at the local high school.

Become a pro wrestler? That would have been like reading comic books and then all of a sudden deciding to become a super-hero. It wasn't even on my radar as a real possibility.

There was only one person I knew who even came close to matching my obsession with pro wrestling. Around 1985, just as WrestleMania and the whole Rock 'n' Wrestling Connection were heating up in the WWF, I became really good friends with a kid at school named Justin. While I had been running CWA tournaments at my house, Justin was busy organizing his own little toy wrestling promotion. (Sadly, neither of us can remember what his organization was called.) I'd go over to Justin's house, and he'd have his guys and I'd have my guys, and we'd pit them against each other in these cross-promotional matches.

Hanging out at Justin's house was a major highlight of my childhood. We got along really well and had a lot of similar interests. Besides the fun of our promotional rivalry, he was also really into video games and had every system imaginable. Meanwhile, I had my cousin's hand-me-down ColecoVision. *Mr. Do,* anybody!?

Justin's mom wasn't especially hands-on when it came to raising him. She had Justin when she was pretty young, so in some ways, she was still kind of off doing her own thing. Luckily, Justin was a smart kid, so he was pretty adept at raising himself.

For me, that meant that when I stayed over at his house, there was no one to tell us to go to bed, no one to tell us we'd been playing video games for way too long, and no one to scold us for prank calling people non-stop.

And the freedom that Justin enjoyed extended to food. Nobody was cooking for Justin. Most of the time, he was heating his own stuff up in the microwave. And his mom bought him really fun, name-brand food, like Reser's Burritos and actual Fruit Loops (instead of the generic "Fruity Rings")—the kind of stuff we rarely saw at my house.

Justin and I would be playing video games, or playing with our wrestling guys, or gambling basketball cards on games of H.O.R.S.E., all while munching on some sweet-ass microwave burritos. Then we'd wake up in the morning, microwave some breakfast sandwiches, and do it all over again.

That processed frozen microwaved garbage Justin and I used to eat as kids is the exact opposite of the kinds of food I choose to eat nowadays. I'll admit that crap still sounds good to me from time to time. But really, that's just nostalgia talking. We all romanticize the foods we loved as kids.

The truth is that all of those 'fun' microwaved foods contain ingredients that, in my opinion, no parent should want their children to ingest, even on a semi-regular basis. But when I was a kid, all those TV commercials were telling me and a bunch of other kids like me that Hot Pockets were the holy grail of food. And as far as I can recall, no one was making much of an effort to teach us different. I don't think most of our parents even realized just how terrible all that frozen food really was.

Food and nutrition were not exactly points of emphasis in school, either. There was always plenty of time for our teachers to teach us skills that no one ever uses in real life, like calculus and geometry. I remember one time, when I was maybe 13 years old, they sent a letter home from school saying I needed a graphing calculator. The thing cost about a hundred bucks.

My dad took one look at the letter, then looked at me and said, "Well, you better get a job." My mom tried to stick up for me. It wasn't like I was dying to get my hands on this calculator. But dad stuck to his guns, and that's how I got my first job, delivering newspapers to pay for a god damn calculator that I have never used since.

I don't know about you, but for all the time we spent in school learning skills that I have never used once outside of a classroom, I was never made to feel that the food I chose to eat was an important building block of my life.

We spent a lot of time worrying about the square root of pi. But in the real world, it turns out I could have used a little information about what's inside apple pie instead.

It's genuinely baffling to me that we don't give schoolkids the basic information they need to make intelligent choices about food. We all have to eat three times a day, every day. It's a pretty big part of our lives. So would it have been so hard for teachers to have brought a bunch of store-bought food products into the classroom, flipped over the packages, and explained what the hell all that information on the back of the packages meant? What are all those words in the ingredients list? What are my daily allowances of things like carbohydrates, protein and fat? What's a real portion size? In the most basic terms: What should I be looking for from food? What should I try to avoid? And why should I even care?

I'm not saying I would have listened. But they could have tried to put the importance of nutrition on my radar. At least then I might have been equipped with a little bit of useful information moving forward. That's the whole point of school, isn't it?

No one teaches you that stuff. I guess you're supposed to figure it out on your own. But how many people actually do? Just to pick one example, off the top of your head, do you have any idea what your maximum daily allowance of sugar should be?

If your answer is no, don't feel bad. You're not alone. Until I took it upon myself to seek out some information, I sure as hell didn't know.

(According to the American Heart Association's 2009 Scientific Statement, the maximum sugar intake per day should be about 6 teaspoons for adult women and 9 teaspoons for adult men.

To put that in perspective, the typical 12oz soda has 8 teaspoons of sugar in it.)

I still remember when the teachers in middle school had to put a limit on how many chocolate chip cookies kids were allowed to buy in the cafeteria. They were the gooey, fresh-baked kind. The cafeteria staff even had a little oven they rolled into the lunchroom and sold the cookies from. They were still warm when you got them. No kid could possibly say no to that.

And sure enough, during lunchtime there would be a huge line of us waiting to get our greasy paws on those greasy cookies. When you peeled one of them up off your napkin, there would be a big stain where it had been. They were disgustingly good, and pretty much exactly what you should not be feeding a bunch of kids at lunch.

I think the cookies cost 45 cents apiece. Some kids would spend almost the whole five bucks they had for lunch money and get 10 cookies. And then they would wash those down with some chocolate milk. That was their whole meal.

Nowadays, we hear a lot about kids having ADD. I don't discount the validity of that disorder, but maybe there's also another culprit to blame. I'm just saying that maybe enabling kids to down copious amounts of sugar at lunch, then sending them back to class and expecting them to sit still and focus might be a problem. It certainly isn't a recipe for maximizing academic achievement.

(I used to have a lot of trouble staying focused in school. Nowadays, I'd probably be diagnosed with ADD. But back then, if you didn't sit still and pay attention like your teacher told you to, you'd have to stay after school. And then you were late coming home. And then your mom would whoop your ass for getting detention. After that happened a few times, you'd learn to control yourself better. That was the old school way they used to treat ADD. But that's a whole other tangent. Let's get back to the topic at hand.)

In high school, I think we spent one semester covering the food pyramid, and that was that. And even that precious food pyramid went out the window as soon as you left the classroom and headed downstairs to the cafeteria. All they ever had there was pizza and burgers and fries and soda and cookies and ice cream. There might have been a salad, but I don't really remember anyone eating one. And besides, if you broke down what was in that salad, it probably wasn't all that healthy anyway.

As I got older, I developed into a pretty good baseball player. But if my high school coaches had any nutritional direction to offer a growing athlete, it was only the most basic health class type of advice: Eat your fruits and vegetables. Don't pig out on candy. And so on. But then at baseball team functions, we always ate pizza and pop and chips and crap like that.

I do remember hearing a lot about milk. That was the one piece of advice adults did bring up. Drink milk for calcium. It's good for your bones. Slam a big glass of milk. And while you're at it, have one of those 50 cent cafeteria ice cream sandwiches, too.

I don't want to sound like I'm being critical of my baseball coaches, or my high school teachers, or my parents, or Justin's mom, or anybody. We're all products of our environment, and the lessons I learned (or didn't learn) about food were the same ones that the adults in my life had learned when they were my age.

People were trying to do the right thing for kids. They were just operating with limited information, bad information, or no information at all.

Like a lot of you reading this book, in the world where I grew up, people only asked a couple questions about food. Was it affordable? Was it easy to make? Did it taste good? And if the answer to all three of those questions was yes, then that's all anyone needed to know.

That's the way things were. For the most part, when I was a kid, I didn't think about the food environment I was raised in any more or less than most people do.

Although in retrospect, one memory does stand out.

When I was young, on Sundays we used to go visit my other grandparents, from my father's side, to share a meal and watch the Packers play.

Grandpa Manny fought in the Korean War, then came home and married Grandma Mary Jo, and together they raised six kids on a small family farm. That was the family side business my dad grew up around.

Grandpa Manny was pretty stern, but Grandma Mary Jo was the one you really didn't mess with. I guess that's the way it had to be when all six of your kids are troublemakers. (If I'm any indication, apparently it runs in the family.)

One of those Sundays, when I was maybe seven or eight years old, I remember going outside to look at Grandpa Manny's cows and feeding them some grass through the fence.

I was looking at this one cow, and the cow was looking at me. And while we were making that eye contact, all of a sudden I felt a little bit of a connection, I guess you'd call it.

It suddenly dawned on me that the cow was a living creature. It was breathing, just like me. And thinking. And feeling. It had emotions. She didn't speak human and I don't speak cow. But other than that, I realized we were really pretty similar.

And then I got called back inside for dinner. The food was already on the table. My family had grilled Italian sausages and brats. I began to eat, but as I chewed that sausage, something felt weird. At that moment, I started connecting the dots. The food I was eating was made out of the same stuff as that cow I had just been mind-melding with outside. I might as well have been eating that very same animal.

Don't get me wrong. I still ate dinner that night. That's what we did. That's the food we ate. That was just the way it was. In my family, you raised the animal, and then you killed it, and then you threw it on the grill. That lifestyle was passed down from my grandfather to my dad and then on to me.

I doubt my grandfather or my father ever had any second thoughts about eating meat. When you rely on a farm for your livelihood, you look at animals differently than most people do. Animals are how you make your money. They're how you put food on the table. That's true both literally and figuratively, because if you don't eat the animals you raise directly, you're going to sell them and get your food money that way. So you view animals as a means to an end and not much more.

I didn't say a word at dinner that day. Even after that incident, when we went home, I didn't take any dramatic stand on eating meat. I don't think I was even capable of realizing that eating meat (or not eating it) was something you *could* take a stand on. It was just a personal gut reaction—all of a sudden, eating cows seemed a bit odd to me.

You might say the first little seed of doubt had been planted in my mind. That's all it was at the time—one little seed.

Hunting and fishing are obviously a big deal in the Midwest. That's probably the case anywhere in America or Canada that's not a city, I guess. Personally, I never really got into either.

For starters, hunting and fishing weren't huge in my family. As I recall, the closest my dad got to hunting was this one time in our backyard, back when I was little. I had this mini Mountain Dew baseball bat we'd gotten at a Brewers game, and I was playing ball, all by myself.

My dad walked up to me.

"Let me see your bat for a minute," he said.

He took that bat, walked to the other side of the yard, and calmly used it to kill a possum that he'd trapped for fucking with his garden. Then he headed back over, gave me my bat back, and walked away. I was four, maybe five years old.

I do recall eating deer meat one time. My uncle had gone hunting and brought the deer back with him. It didn't taste good to me at all. Truthfully, I thought it was disgusting. There wasn't much chance of me spending all day in the woods with a rifle just so I could come home with more of that.

During deer season in Wisconsin, you see lots of cars with a deer or two strapped to their roofs. Visually, it's pretty in your face.

Deer hunters are often quick to tell you about deer overpopulation, and why humans need to kill so many of them each year. I'm sure there's some substance to that, although as far as I've seen, deer are pretty docile. They don't really mess with anybody. I sure don't see them overtaking humankind anytime soon.

When people get passionate about why we need to kill all the deer, to me, sometimes they sound kind of defensive. It seems like they might just be clinging to a justification that lets them go kill a bunch of stuff and then go home with a clear conscience. That's how it can come across to me, anyway.

I did try fishing, but that wasn't my thing either. Everyone loves to tell you how relaxing it is to go fishing. Well, sure it's relaxing—until it's time to pull some fish out of the water who clearly does not want to be hooked on your line. And then you have to decide whether to throw the fish back in or kill it.

As soon as I saw a fish on my hook, I immediately felt bad. The fish was obviously not getting any enjoyment out of the experience. And I could relate. How would I like it if someone dangled some delicious pie in front of my face, and then as soon as I took a bite, hooked me through the mouth and yanked me out of my front door? Even if they decided to throw me back in because I wasn't big enough, that seems like it would be pretty traumatic.

Even as a little kid, the whole process of fishing seemed a bit cruel. Just like seeing all those deer hanging off of all those cars.

I remember trying to put myself in the animals' shoes, so to speak. Imagine how cool it would be to be a bird, and to be able to fly. Except one day, you're up there soaring around, not bothering anybody, and then boom, you get shot out of the sky. Or imagine if you were a fish chilling in a lake, but when you moseyed over to nibble on a snack, you ended up with a hook poking out of your cheek.

Where I grew up, hunting and fishing were supposed to be "normal." But from as far back as I can remember, just like the thought of eating one of Grandpa Manny's cows, the thought of doing either of them didn't sit quite right with me.

Compared to a lot of the kids I grew up with, I think it was always in my nature to think outside the box.

Life was good in Waukesha. Compared to lots of other places on the globe where I could have grown up, I hit the jackpot, and I know it.

But life there was also very average. It was very normal. In places like Waukesha—and there are tons of them, all over the world—there's a definite path laid out for you. And everyone knows what it is from the time they're born. You go to school. You get good grades. You go to college, if you can, or you get a job. Then you settle down and have kids, usually within a 25-mile radius of where you grew up. And that's it.

There's nothing at all wrong with that. My sister Diana embraced that path. She wanted that stability. So she got good grades, worked hard to get her degree, became a teacher and ended up married to a neighbor of ours from when we were kids. They have two sons, two dogs, and a happy, normal home. That works for her, and I love visiting them and experiencing that life when I can.

But from a very young age, I knew I wanted something different. I wanted to get out and do some exploring.

Neither of my parents had gone to college. But I was in a position to go, and when I graduated from high school, that's what they wanted me to do.

Baseball was supposed to be my ticket. I grew up playing the usual all-American sports, the same as most other kids. But for whatever reason, I ended up being really good at baseball. I was a crafty left-handed pitcher and a speedy center fielder.

I wouldn't say I ever truly loved baseball. I mean, I really liked it and I enjoyed playing it. I followed the Brewers and the Chicago Cubs, thanks to afternoon games and a drunken Harry Caray doing play-by-play. I also think that when you're good at a sport and people encourage you to develop your talent, that naturally raises your interest. But I never had a burning passion for the game—at least not like I did for pro wrestling.

The way my dad saw it, my talent for baseball would allow me go to college, get a degree, get a job, start a family, and then work my ass off for the next 50 years. It didn't matter what line of work I got into. My dad wasn't the kind of guy who was going to tell me I could be anything I wanted to be if I just put my mind to it.

My mom was the more open-minded of my two parents. She encouraged me to make my own decisions and to pursue things that would make me happy. Later on, after college, when I spent a few years doing things that weren't exactly law-abiding or intelligent, she still tried to be supportive. In her mind, once I was out on my own, I was on my own. She wasn't going to tell me how to live my life.

But my dad had a very conservative, straightforward, old school mentality. He had worked all kinds of jobs to support us. And remember, he had been raised on Grandpa Manny's farm, baling hay and all that. When my dad was a kid, after school was done for the day, he didn't come home and play *Farmville* on Facebook. He did actual farm work.

That's what needed to be done. That's how the family made money. And that instilled a work ethic in my dad that he tried to pass down to me, all the way back to my paper route and that god damn graphing calculator.

By the time I graduated from high school, I didn't know what I wanted to be when I grew up. I just knew I didn't want to be normal. I wanted more from life than the mundane nine-to-five existence I saw all around me.

But I didn't exactly have any alternate plan lined up to throw back at my dad. I didn't know yet that I wanted to be a wrestler. Plus, to be fair, it sounded kind of exciting to go play college baseball and in the process get a degree that might help me make some money someday.

So when it came time for college, I did things my dad's way. I got a few scholarship offers to play ball. And in the end, off I went to Winona State University, a few hours from home, in Winona, Minnesota.

Although in retrospect I had no idea where my life was ultimately headed, at the time I was excited to go away to school. I was excited to get out on my own and live on a college campus. I was excited to join the team. But looking back, I was probably just as excited to jump into the whole college social experience.

The reality is, when you get to the college level, baseball becomes a full-time commitment. Outside of studying, you need to make practicing and playing ball the focal point of your whole life. Baseball needs to become your identity. There's nothing wrong with that. That's the deal.

But then, of course, on your first day at school you're standing outside smoking a cig, just taking it all in, and a car rolls up. Someone calls you over and asks if you want to go to a party that night. And, of course, you say, "Yes!"

And in my case, at least, when you go to that party, that same guy also asks you if you want a fake ID. And if you want to help him sell fake IDs to all the other new freshman on campus, too. And then before you know it, you're at baseball practice all day, and at night you're walking into a bar for the $4 all-you-can-drink special, thanks to an ID that says you're a 33-year-old man.

By the time I left high school, I had picked up some typical teenage habits that don't lend themselves to athletic excellence. If my friends and I could get our hands on alcohol, we'd drink. I had long ago started smoking cigarettes and drinking coffee, so if the weekend came and there wasn't any booze available, we'd spend Friday night at a bakery shop pounding coffee and chain smoking. I was also dabbling with different party drugs.

So right from the start of college, I was getting pulled in two different directions: I was caught between having a good time and dedicating the proper time and attention to baseball.

To make matters worse, I still didn't possess any real knowledge about the kind of lifestyle a developing athlete is supposed to follow. I can still remember the feeling I had the first time I walked into a college weight room.

This was before tryouts and before I even met my future teammates. The gym was much bigger than the one at my high school. And everyone there was much bigger than me, too. You're talking about experienced college athletes who are 20 or 21. Meanwhile, I'm this clueless scrawny 17-year-old.

It's overwhelming. You see all the other guys in there, and they all know what they're doing, and you have almost no clue. So you do a couple of reps with the first piece of equipment that looks somewhat familiar, you hope no one is staring at you, and then you get the hell out of there as soon as possible.

Looking back, I think I may have felt defeated before I even got started. That right there might have been the beginning of the end for me and America's Pastime.

I think I also had some trouble fitting in with guys who identified solely as baseball players. I've always tried to avoid being labeled or pigeon-holed as a person. Even though I was good enough to play at the college level, I didn't consider myself a jock. Unlike the rest of the players, I didn't walk around wearing Nike shoes and my baseball jacket 24-7. I had my ears pierced five times, plus my labret and my tongue, too. And as a result, I felt like a bit of a social outcast on the team.

Almost immediately, baseball changed from something that was fun into a chore. The tipping point might have been when I was tasked with selling a ridiculous amount of these Scandinavian pastries known as kringles as a fundraiser.

Even though I made the varsity team my freshman year, before the season started, I decided to walk away. I told the administrators I wanted to focus more on my studies. I might have even told myself the same thing. But in reality, I just wanted to focus on going out and partying.

I fell immediately and completely into the typical unhealthy college lifestyle. There was the drinking and the marijuana. And I quickly discovered new and exciting uses for Reddi-Wip. In short, I went from being a varsity college baseball player to being a beer league softball all-star.

When you live at home with your parents, there's a certain amount of order to your life. You take it for granted that the toilet paper is going to be on the roll and that there's always a full tube of toothpaste. Then you go away to school and all of that order instantly vanishes. You need a game plan for your daily life, and, to put it mildly, I didn't have one.

One of the basic freedoms that come with college life is the freedom to choose whatever food you want to eat. Unfortunately, at most colleges that means young people are free to choose from among the worst foodstuffs legally available in America. Everyone talks about college kids drinking too much. But when people talk about gaining the Freshman Fifteen, you don't hear quite as much about the awful food.

Of course, there were the notoriously terrible dining options in the cafeteria. Most college freshmen don't have a lot of disposable income, and whatever money they do have usually goes to alcohol and maybe weed or other drugs. That's why they all eat at the cafeteria. You get your cafeteria meal plan for the year, and it's a free pass to eat whatever you want, and as much as you want, day in and day out.

And the choices there are just as bad as they were in the high school cafeteria. It's the exact same shit—chicken patties, grilled cheese, pizza, burgers, pizza burgers, and so on. And the nutritional content is poor, even by the standards of regular burgers and chicken patties. But those are your choices.

I remember loading my plate up with these disgusting cafeteria grilled cheese sandwiches, then ladling a few spoonfuls of cafeteria chili on top of them. That was a go-to treat throughout my freshman year (and ironically, in some small way, the beginning my culinary creativity).

To make matters worse, that garbage is the only food you ever eat. At least in high school, when you go home for dinner, your parents might try to make you eat a somewhat healthy meal. But in college, the leash is off entirely.

My freshman year, I remember I stayed in the dorm over Christmas. The cafeteria was closed for the holidays, and at one point I decided I couldn't stomach yet another serving of instant ramen. So following my culinary muse, I headed down to the vending machine, and voila, a handful of change later, I had invented something I liked to call Crunchy Chili Cheese Cool Ranch Funyun Ramen Delight. Boom—problem solved.

Of course, it was possible to buy food off campus. But Winona was a small town. There are maybe 25,000 people total, and college students probably make up a third of that. In a town that size, the options were limited.

Dominos became a frequent late night event. Thin crust pizza was cheaper, so I used to get that with sausage. I'd fold two slices together like a sandwich and then dip them in ranch.

And then there was a Hardee's, conveniently located right on the walk from the campus to the downtown area. I used to pop in there and gulp down a couple of hot ham and Swiss sandwiches on my way to or from the bars.

Looking back, that kind of diet seems completely ridiculous to me. Don't get me wrong. I'm not a saint. To this day, I still indulge in food that isn't great for me. But nowadays, it's hard to fathom the things I consistently chose to wolf down back then. And I'm not just talking about the calories, but the actual quality of the food—or lack thereof. And I didn't just do that once or twice. It was all the time.

But my eating habits weren't all that unusual. If you went to college, you know—that's just what college kids eat: stuff that's convenient and greasy and shitty.

I've held on to the checkbook I kept during my freshman year of college, just to remind myself how incredibly misguided I was at that time. My financial aid package included some extra money to cover my living expenses. If you look through that old checkbook, you'll see a deposit for a couple grand from financial aid, and then you'll see all the transactions going to the same couple of fast food spots and watering holes. Dominos. Bullseye Beer Hall. The local liquor store. Those same three places, over and over and over again.

Right after I got a check, the money would be flying out. Then it would slow down to a trickle as my funds ran low, until there were just a few dollars left. I remember writing a $6 check to Bullseye once, leaving me with exactly $1.42 in my account. Eventually, I'd get a fresh transfusion of financial aid funds, and then the process would repeat itself again.

Sophomore year, I moved off campus and into downtown Winona. I was in a little apartment, conveniently located directly above a bar.

I no longer had to live on cafeteria food. But that didn't necessarily mean my diet improved. I can remember convincing myself that a Sunday morning Bloody Mary kind of counted as food, because of the olives, pickles, and the celery. Add in a one-dollar bag of chips or peanuts, and there you go—breakfast is served.

Since I now had a kitchen in my apartment, and since I was in a constant cash crunch, I learned to cook a little bit out of necessity. But just because I started preparing my own food doesn't mean I was learning to eat any better. I figured out that melting my own hot ham and cheese sandwiches was cheaper than buying them at Hardee's. I used to make chilidogs in my apartment, too, and I ate a ton of three-for-a-dollar boxes of mac and cheese.

But I still didn't have any real dietary tools or information to fall back on. I went for the foods I knew, and that I liked, and that I could afford. That's as far as my thought process went. Any consideration of whether the food I was eating was good or bad for me didn't enter the equation in the slightest.

I have a picture of myself from my sophomore or junior year. If you look at me, the first thing you'll notice is what my nose looked like before I broke it a dozen times. But then you'll also notice that I'm what you might call "skinny fat." I wasn't humongous. I was born with a really high metabolism. To this day, I have a hard time keeping on weight. At the peak of my skinny fat era, I probably topped out at about 165 pounds.

But I had gotten a fat face. I was doughy to the touch. I was soft. Even though I didn't have a gut, I guarantee you my body fat percentage was high for my body size. Here I was, a guy who had been recruited to play baseball only a couple years before this picture was taken, and now, suddenly, I had no chin.

A lot of people choose to glamorize this type of down and dirty college lifestyle. But looking back, that life was kind of sad compared to how many better things I could have been doing with my time.

Like so many other young people at that stage of life, I was trying to find myself. I was afraid that if I wasn't out at the bars with everybody else, I might miss out on something. In reality, 99.9% of what happens in college bars is all the same and a massive waste of time. When you spend all your time there, you're actually missing out on all the really cool life experiences that are happening almost everywhere else—except for inside those dark, loud, smelly shitholes.

One night, I was so desperate to get my $4 all-you-can-drink Red Solo cup down at the bar I sold my roommate a Jenny McCarthy poster.

"You mean the one that's already hanging on the wall in the room I already live in?" he asked.

"Well, yeah," I replied in my best used car salesman pitch. "But you get to take it home with you at the end of the year!"

And yes, he did give me five bucks for the poster. Out of pity, I guess.

Another time, during my freshman year, Grandpa Gerd and Grandma Ginny drove out to Winona for a visit. I took them out to a local bar and proudly ordered my Grandpa his favorite drink, a Southern Comfort Manhattan with a cherry. I got my Grandma a Fuzzy Navel.

I think Grandma and Grandpa started to realize something was up when the bartender told us the first round was on the house.

My grandparents said, "Wait, you're only 18. Aren't you too young to be in a bar?"

That's when I pointed out my name written up on the wall. I had been away at school for all of three months, but I had already scored a free $150 bar tab as my reward for winning the Bar Olympics.

(Take that, Kurt Angle. You won a gold medal with a broken frickin' neck? Well, I won the Bar Olympics with a wicked frickin' hangover.)

Completing the Winona State equivalent of the Triple Crown, I later won the Valentine's Day Make-Out Contest at that same bar and was crowned Karaoke Champion for my stirring rendition of "My Own Prison" by Creed.

(Yeah, I know. Creed sucks. But back then, for a couple months there, everyone thought Scott Stapp was cool, before the world figured out that he's a head case.)

During my sophomore year, I got a job working at a pizzeria called Giovanni's. I loved pizza, and I needed the money, so the job was a win-win.

This was right when the NWO was hot and the WWF's Attitude

Era was happening. Ironically, although I never stopped following wrestling, during the Monday Night Wars—when pro wrestling exploded back into the mainstream—my interest in the sport dipped to an all-time low.

As a broke college kid, I didn't have cable, so I couldn't watch wrestling at my house. But that wasn't the main reason I had kind of checked out.

Suddenly, out of nowhere, Mondays turned into a really busy night for pizza deliveries. I'd go out to frat houses that were having these big get-togethers, all so a bunch of meatheads who hadn't followed wrestling since Hulkamania could watch *Raw* and *Nitro,* drink a ton of beer, and send each other Too Sweets and People's Eyebrows.

That got under my skin. I'd loved wrestling since I was little. I'd never stopped. But for a long time, it had been what you might call a secret passion. Before the Attitude Era heated up, once you were approaching manhood, it wasn't considered cool to follow pro wrestling. It wasn't something you publically advertised.

So although I mostly kept it to myself, while I loved the Attitude Era, it also kind of pissed me off. I felt like it attracted a bunch of bandwagon jumpers who didn't really respect wrestling. They were just watching it because crotch chopping suddenly became the cool thing to do.

It's like if you're a hardcore Misfits fan, and then you see someone walk out of Hot Topic with a Misfits shirt. It's easy to resent that person, because you feel like they're just attaching themselves to a trendy logo when that logo actually means something to you. You wonder if that person can even name a single Misfits song.

Eventually, my car broke down, so I had to quit my job delivering pizzas. There was a liquor store across the street from my apartment that owned their own delivery truck, so I went to work for them instead.

Meanwhile, my college career entered a slow, gradual decline.

School had always come easy to me. I always got good grades without really trying. But in this new environment, I found that I wasn't motivated to make much of an effort. I just wasn't in a place in my life where getting grades or learning in that type of environment was important to me.

In college you have to self-motivate. Unlike when you're in high school, there's nobody there to tell you to get out of bed in the morning and go to class. There's no principal to punish you if you don't. There's no one leaning on you to do your homework. You either make yourself do it or it doesn't get done.

I wasn't learning all that much, and now that I was paying to go to school, I couldn't wrap my brain around all the bullshit mandatory classes I was forced to take as part of my school's core curriculum. The whole thing started to feel like one big scam.

At first, my grades were good. Then they weren't so good. Then there were some classes I had to take a second time.

My last year, I signed up for a bunch of classes, but then as soon as I got my financial aid money, I dropped them all. I just needed that three grand to live on. (Of course, it never crossed my mind that someday I was going to have to pay all that money back, with interest.)

I had gone to college because that's what I was told I was supposed to do and because baseball had opened doors for me. But now that baseball was gone, I discovered that I couldn't find a good reason to be there.

There wasn't a whole lot going on in my life. I was stuck in a meaningless pattern of alcohol, drugs, terrible food and hanging out in bars.

After a couple of years spent trying to convince myself that I should stick it out, I realized that if my heart wasn't into going to college, then I was just wasting my time and my money. So I made the decision to break up with college.

We both knew it was time.

CHAPTER 2

Looking back, the end of my college days turned out to be the darkness before the dawn. But it took some time before I started to see the light and get my life on track.

Once I cut ties with college, I found myself in no man's land. According to society, going to college is the right thing to do. We congratulate kids for heading off to college, even if they have no idea why they're going there, what they want to study, or what they're planning to do once they get that diploma.

But when college didn't work out, there wasn't any obvious move for me to make next. There aren't a lot of socially acceptable game plans for college dropouts.

I didn't know what I was looking for. All I knew was that, whatever it was, I wasn't going to find it in Winona, Minnesota or Waukesha, Wisconsin.

I had to change my environment. So I hit the road.

One of the fringe benefits of working at that pizza place in Winona was that my shift manager, Steve, became my marijuana hook-up. (Steve was more than just a co-worker. He became a friend, and still is to this day. Now that he's a respectable adult, I've changed his name so the people who know him today don't realize that he used to be a bit of a Heisenberg back then.)

As I got to know Steve, I came to realize that he was no nickel and dime-bag weed source. Actually, he was the biggest marijuana supplier for all of Winona. And as it turned out as he got to know me, he had some use for my services.

At first, I just started off storing some of his product in the closets at my off-campus apartment. But then, once I quit pretending I was going to school and my schedule opened up, Steve was more than happy to get a responsible Caucasian male with a clean record more involved in his operation.

So I became his partner of sorts. In addition to being the storage facility, I also became the means of transportation. I started making runs down to Steve's suppliers in the Southwest.

You might say I headed out on the road because I was trying to find myself and that I was looking to sow some of my wild oats, so to speak. And that would be true. But more importantly, without those financial aid checks coming in, I was also trying to figure out a way to make some quick money and keep myself afloat.

Through working for Steve, I came into contact with a guy called Crazy T. Crazy T had a shaggy mop of hair and a long goatee. He also had two of his canines filed down into fangs. CT was probably in his late thirties at the time. That seemed ancient to me, even though that's how old I am now.

Crazy T and his partner owned a blown glass company. They supplied custom glass bongs and other pieces to a lot of the big bands and artists around at the time.

Unlike the cliché of the lazy stoner, CT was super hyperactive. While his partner would stay back and handle the business side of things, CT would travel all over and hit up a bunch of events—concerts, the Warped Tour, the upstart X-Games, whatever big thing was going on. With endless energy, he'd hand out business cards and show off his glass pieces to try to make new connections. Ideally, he'd sell some of his pieces, too, but if not, CT always had something he could flip to make some cash.

Since we had some mutual business interests and contacts, CT and I started spending a lot of time together driving around and shooting the shit.

Before I started making these cross-country runs, I had never stepped foot outside of the Midwest. Minnesota was the farthest I had ever been away from Wisconsin, and it's the next state over.

But now, I was driving to spots like San Diego, Phoenix and Venice Beach. I didn't have anything else going on in my life, so I ended up spending almost three straight months with CT, living on floors, blow-up mattresses, and couches and bouncing from place to place.

CT was a really intense, in-your-face kind of guy, and boy, could he talk. He was always telling these crazy-ass stories. When he found out I was into wrestling, for example, he told me about the time "Macho Man" Randy Savage had tried to talk him into becoming a pro wrestler.

You could never be sure if CT even believed half of what was coming out of his mouth. But he'd never let you know that, and he never ran out of material.

Here's the kind of guy we're talking about: One time, out of nowhere, Crazy T decided that we needed a Jeep. I don't know why, but as soon as the idea popped into his mind, it became his number one priority. So that same afternoon, CT walked into a dealership, dropped 15 grand in cash, and drove off in his new blue Jeep Wrangler. To put things in perspective, at that time my car was probably worth about $1,500.

And then as soon as CT got the Jeep, he started talking me into buying some deluxe $100 sleeping bag.

"Look, bro," he said. "What if we're in the desert with the Jeep and we need to sleep out there? It gets really cold at night and you're going to need one."

So I bought the sleeping bag. I think the thing is rated to -100 degrees. It's still in my closet. To this day, I've never used it once.

CT was always going on about one thing or another.

"Bro, you gotta stop eating that red meat and that pork. I'm telling you, that shit's no good for you."

I don't know exactly how Crazy T had arrived at this opinion.

I just know that, like a lot of his opinions, he felt very strongly about it. I remember CT saying that John Wayne died of colon cancer. He claimed that The Duke had gotten cancer because he ate too much beef. Other than that one bit of information (which might not have even been true, for all I knew), I don't think there were a whole lot of facts to back up CT's argument. To him, I think it was just an obvious fact. Red meat and pork were bad for you. That was that.

Until the moment Crazy T brought it up, I don't think it had ever occurred to me that meat could be bad for you. Sure, too much ice cream's bad for you. Candy's bad for you. Everybody knows that. But beef? Pork?

Obviously, I didn't swear off hamburgers on the spot. But looking back, just like that one day, long ago, hanging out with that cow at my Grandpa Manny's farm, another small seed was planted in my mind.

Another time, CT and I were driving through Texas, passing through a big stretch of long flat nothingness, when we came upon a huge slaughterhouse. I was blown away by the sheer size of the place. We kept driving and driving, and the slaughterhouse kept coming and coming. It stretched out for a mile at least. I had never seen anything like it.

Until that moment, my mental image of where meat came from was based on my grandparents' farm. At the height of that farm, before I was born, Grandpa Manny and Grandma Mary Jo had probably kept about a dozen chickens and half a dozen cows at any given time. By the time I came around, they had maybe half that.

There was nothing evil or industrial about their farm. It was a pretty mellow little spot. And that was what I had in mind when I ate cows and chickens and eggs. I think that's where a lot of people imagine their meat comes from.

But the factory chicken farm I was now driving past was nothing like Grandpa Manny's and Grandma Mary Jo's. It was big and dirty and smelly, and it was hard to imagine that anything good was going on inside it.

It seemed like there was a dark cloud hanging over the whole area. I believe in karma or energy or whatever you want to call it. And this place had some seriously bad juju.

I don't recall CT and I having a conversation about that slaughterhouse. But the image lingered in my mind for a long time afterward.

In retrospect, that was another little seed.

Eventually, CT and I wound up in Lake Havasu, where we fell into a daily routine: After sleeping on some buddies' couches, we would wake up about 9AM. We'd go hang out on the lake in our friend's boat, burn some bud, drink a few beers, and maybe do a little wakeboarding. In the afternoon, while the other guys worked their telemarketing jobs, CT and I would grab some food or take a nap. Once those guys finished work, we'd all go hit the club and drink some vodka Red Bulls. Then we'd go to an after-hours place, close that down, get home around 4AM, and crash on the couch. Then the next day we'd do it all over again.

It was the same thing, day after day, for about two months straight. I might have been wasting my time, but I was having a helluva good time doing it.

Without even trying to, I was starting to eat a little better. Compared to all the big corporate fast food chains in my college town, the options in Lake Havasu tended to be a little healthier.

CT was the guy with the money, so he made a lot of the decisions. Since he had his stance about beef and pork, I started eating a lot of chicken. I was never a big red meat and pork guy anyway. I liked my Whoppers with Cheese as much as the next guy, but chicken wraps and chicken sandwiches were fine with me, too.

Pretty soon, I barely ate any meat other than chicken. And I can't say that I missed anything. In the big picture, those chicken wraps probably weren't all that healthy. But compared to

Hardee's hot ham and cheeses and those cafeteria grilled cheese sandwiches smothered in chili, they were at least a couple steps in the right direction.

Thanks to the wakeboarding, plus biking, hiking, and walking more, I was more active than I had been in Winona, so I was getting in shape a bit. Now that I was away from the Midwest winters and out in the sun, I was getting a nice tan, too. I had just gotten my Kanji ram tattoo. (CT traded a tattoo artist a glass bong in exchange for some ink on my arm as a gift for my 22nd birthday.)

My hair was getting pretty long. Looking back, my 'do looked a little bit like Dragon Ball Z. All in all, though, for a skinny fat guy, I looked kind of badass. Okay, maybe not badass, but definitely not Midwest normal.

As you might have guessed by now, by this time I had started experimenting with some psychedelic drugs. People can say what they want about drugs. And I'm certainly not going to say that drugs are good for you.

But in my experience, under the right circumstances, at the right time in your life, some drugs can help open certain parts of your brain and help you see things from a whole new perspective. Even the morning after, once the drugs wear off, they can still leave a lasting impression that you take with you moving forward. That's how they worked for me, anyway.

At one point, while under the influence of some chemical enhancement, I remember finding myself on a boat out in the middle of Lake Havasu surrounded by all these random people I had just met. And I got to thinking.

Where I grew up, everything had been very plain and predictable. There's a certain way you're expected to live your life, and very few people deviate from the blueprint. But now, I was mingling with people who operated way outside of the norm—and made it work for them. I had just spent some time in Flagstaff, Arizona, for example, hanging out with these super cool hippie artists who all lived in a house together and made blown glass all day. They seemed free from so many of the typical societal shackles.

And at that moment, chilling on that boat, I realized just how far away I was from the world I grew up in. There were kids I went to high school with who were never going to venture outside Waukesha. And there were people I knew at those college bars who were going to get swallowed up by Winona and never leave.

It was depressing to ponder how so many people, from my perspective, had been led onto a path to nowhere. But it was also inspiring to realize that I didn't have to be one of them.

I had wasted a bunch of money going to college. But now that I was traveling and exploring and meeting new people, I was finally starting to learn something.

I realized that the ball was in my court. I had the option of doing what society had groomed me to do, living the rest of my days feeling resentful and bitter, working a job I didn't like, and then retiring feeling old, defeated, and unhappy. That life was all lined up for me, if I wanted to do what I'd been told. But here I was, away from all that. I felt excited about all the possibilities in front of me. I realized that I was free to do whatever I wanted to do with my life. I could take on any adventure I felt like pursuing.

I just needed to answer some questions: Who was I? What did I stand for? What was I going to be?

I made the decision to move out of the Midwest for good. I didn't have any money or any real direction. I still didn't know where my life was headed. But I knew I was having a lot of fun and meeting all kinds of interesting people. So I decided to pull up stakes and relocate to Lake Havasu.

I was back in Winona packing up my limited earthly possessions when the phone rang. It was my old grade school buddy Justin.

Since I had gone away to college, Justin and I had only been in touch here and there. While I was up in Winona, busy winning the Bar Olympics, Justin moved to Key West for a while before moving to Virginia and working with the band GWAR.

(This was probably 15 years ago. In the beginning, Justin had an entry-level GWAR job as a band slave named Taintmonger selling merch at their shows. Most recently, you could have caught him on the band's last tour, on stage as Gor-Gor the dinosaur.)

I hadn't talked to Justin in a while. But now, he was calling me out of the blue to tell me he was also in Minneapolis, just a couple hours away from Winona.

"Shit, man," I said. "What are you doing up there?"

He told me he was training to be a wrestler.

Justin and I had been big wrestling fans ever since we were kids. Nonetheless, I was floored by what he was telling me. What do you mean you're training to be a wrestler? I mean, who just trains to be a wrestler?

At that point, in my early twenties, I guess I still had never really thought about how someone got started in the wrestling business. Nowadays, you can Google "wrestling school" and 40 of them pop up. But I don't think that was the case in 2000. And if it was, I was definitely not aware of it.

Justin told me he was training with a guy called Eddie Sharkey. Hearing that name told me that Justin's school was legit.

Casual wrestling fans might not know Eddie's name, but within the industry—and to hardcore fans—Eddie is known as "The Trainer of Champions." I had seen his name tons of times over the years in the wrestling magazines. Eddie's been associated with a lot of big names that came out of the Minneapolis area, like Rick Rude, The Repo Man, and X-Pac. To me, Eddie's name carried weight most of all because I knew he had trained The Road Warriors.

If my buddy was training to be a wrestler, well, then, I had to go check it out. So later that week I hopped in my car and headed up to St. Louis Park, Minnesota.

The training facility was located in a two-car garage. The garage was in the back of a house owned by Eddie's partner, Terry Fox.

I walked inside, and, for the first time in my life outside of the Mecca, I saw a real-life wrestling ring. The ring was small—16 foot by 16 foot—and low to the ground. There was enough room on one side of the ring for some chairs or a space heater during those brutal Minnesota winters. But the other three walls were probably within two feet of the ring. If you wanted to try a body slam or a vertical suplex, you had to be careful to make sure no one hit the roof.

But still, holy fuck, there it was—a wrestling ring! Terry's garage wasn't much compared to the places I wrestle nowadays. But at that moment, I was completely in awe.

There were a couple guys working out in the ring when I got there. After watching them for a couple minutes, I could tell they weren't very good. Or at the very least, I knew that I could be better. Hell, I'd delivered better drop kicks to that inner tube in my grandma's pool back when I was four.

Before that moment, I had never felt like I had a clear direction in life. But now, instantly, I knew this was it for me.

So I begged Terry, that first day.

"Terry, please," I said. "Can I get in the ring? I just want to see what it's like."

"Nope," he told me. "It's $3,000. And you gotta sign a waiver."

Wrestling trainers have always wanted to see the money up front. Years later, when I ran the training school for Ring of Honor, I was the same way.

Wrestling has traditionally been a very guarded industry. Before the late 80s, when Vince McMahon admitted that wrestling is entertainment, the whole business was grounded in keeping fans believing that the competition was real.

So back in the day, if a guy showed up at the gym and said he wanted to be a wrestler, the regulars there didn't just wave him on in. They actively tried to weed people out. They only wanted guys who belonged.

A lot of guys think they want to be wrestlers and say they want to be wrestlers, but when push comes to shove, most people can't handle it. The old school approach—which was still in place when I got started—was to beat you up and try to break you and then see if you still come back tomorrow.

That saves everyone a lot of time. That's what the business will do to you eventually. So if you can't handle it, you might as well find that out as soon as possible. They broke Hulk Hogan's leg when he first started out just to see if he would take that punishment and still come back.

It's a lot like magicians. If I tell you how we do all the tricks, you might just go off and tell your friends that magic is bullshit. So before I start giving you the goods, I'm going to need to see you invest some money and time and focus. I can't just get a little down payment from a guy, then bring him in the ring and show him how to do a "Stone Cold Stunner."

If I'm your trainer, for the first month you're not getting in the ring. I want to see your conditioning and what kind of shape you're in, both physically and mentally. If you just showed up to learn a couple moves, after two weeks you'll probably give up and get lost. And then I've got half your money.

That's how it works in wrestling, at least the way I was taught. You're either all the way in or you're out.

On the day I met Terry Fox, I had maybe $500 to my name. But Terry could sense my desire. He could tell how badly I wanted it. He told me that years later.

He added, "I could tell there was just something different about you from the look in your eyes."

Back when I was four years old, remember, I used to take my wrestling figures and give them new names and new looks and new gimmicks. But now, here was a chance to do all that stuff in real life.

So Terry and I worked out a deal. I gave him half the money I had, and I agreed to pay him whatever I could, every week, until the tuition was paid off. To this day, I'm grateful to Terry for making that deal.

Next, I had to work out a deal with Justin. And like a true friend, he made it really easy. Without hesitation, he agreed to let me move in with him until I got my feet on the ground.

My whole life was already packed up back in Winona. But now, instead of heading back to the West Coast and continuing the life I had started out there, I drove up to Minneapolis and moved onto Justin's couch.

As my training got underway, I quickly came to realize that while Eddie Sharkey's name might have been on the school, as Eddie's partner, Terry was doing most of the work.

Terry is a high school janitor by day who runs a wrestling school in his spare time. He doesn't get rich running the place. He does it because he loves wrestling. He loves training guys, and he loves putting on his own shows.

Sometimes, for the hell of it, he throws on a mask and turns into The Masked Jungle Fighter. One time, instead of the mask, he put on a powder blue singlet and a feather boa. Let's just say his "Luscious" Larry Lipton character was so good, for all the wrong reasons.

Terry's got a good heart, and he's always got a smile for you, especially when he's asking if you have the money you owe him. "You got something for me?" That was Terry's famous line when he asked the guys for training dues.

I love Eddie Sharkey, but by the time I came along, Eddie was too old to do much in the ring. Most of the time he would just sit in his chair and tell these far-fetched stories, like the one about the time him and Harley Race got into a bar fight.

"I went to stick my finger in the guy's eye to pull his eyeball out," he'd say. "And all I got was his socket, because Harley beat me to it!"

Unless you've ever felt as rudderless as I did when I left college, or as passionate as I felt when I discovered my path in wrestling, I don't know if I can explain the feeling. I can just tell you that I felt very fortunate to have found a direction in my life. When wrestling found me, I probably wasn't headed down a very good road.

I had always known I wasn't like everyone else. I knew I didn't belong in the normal everyday system. But once I found wrestling, for the first time, I really knew what I was. This was where I belonged.

It felt like someone had plugged me into a wall socket. I was surging with energy around the clock.

Once I found wrestling, my whole life changed course. Little by little, the pieces finally started falling into place. Here's an example of what I'm talking about: Once I started training, I got a gym membership at Bally's. They had a deal where if I made my $60 payment on time every month for 18 months, my payments would then drop to $7 a month.

I knew I needed to keep training. And I knew I had to make every dollar count. So I made the payment on time, every time. As someone with credit card and college loan debt, this was a first. That may sound really insignificant. But back in college, I used to binge and purge my way through those financial aid checks. And now, for the first time since I'd been out on my own, I was getting organized and becoming financially responsible.

I had been quick to give up on the gym at Winona State during my brief time on the baseball team. I was embarrassed by how little I knew about the equipment and how puny I was compared to some of the upperclassmen. But now, giving up was not an option.

So I went on the internet and learned some beginner workout routines. Justin was there to teach me some stuff, and going to the gym together made us push each other harder. (As anyone who's ever visited a gym knows, just because you're there doesn't necessarily mean you're really working out.)

I knew that in order to have a real future in wrestling I had to look the part and put some size on. In my experience, what really sets guys apart on the independent level of wrestling is the dedication they put into their diet and their training.

Early on, you could tell which guys were approaching wrestling as a career and which guys were just doing it as a hobby. I remember one of my favorite guys back then, Dr. Darin Davis. By day, he was a computer programmer. But in the ring, he was everybody's favorite proctologist.

He would usually work shows as a baby face. When the time was right, he'd pull out the latex glove, put it on his hand, and then shove it down the back of the heel's trunks. The opponent would dance around like he had Dr. Darin's hand up his ass. (As we say in the biz: It's not gay. It's pro wrestling.) The crowd loved it.

Dr. Darin Davis wasn't really trying to be on TV or make a career. He was a super nice guy and he understood and respected the business, but he approached wrestling the way some guys approach their Tuesday night softball league. He wasn't going to the gym five nights a week or fine-tuning his diet or taking supplements so he could take himself to the next level. He was happy right where he was.

There are a lot of talented guys who aren't compelled to put the effort in outside the ring, because their end game doesn't require it. Other guys have wrestling as their sole focus and will do everything it takes to make it to the top.

Two guys I came across early on who really embodied that approach were Shawn Daivari and Ken Anderson. Based on the way they carried themselves back then, it's no surprise to me that they've both done great things in the industry. I took one look at those guys and figured, whatever they were doing, that's what I needed to be doing, too.

Once I moved to Minneapolis, suddenly, instantly, training was all that mattered to me. I wasn't thinking about an end game.

I wasn't thinking about winning championship belts in wrestling or being famous or getting on TV. I was just insanely grateful to have this opportunity. So I gave it everything I had.

It was an awesome time, but it was a brutal time, too. Everything revolved around the three days a week I would get to train. I was doing temp jobs when I could to pay Terry my tuition and to help Justin out with some bills. I would show up to Labor-Ready at 4AM hoping to get sent to a work site. Usually, I got sent out on construction jobs.

Between wrestling and construction work and lifting, my body started to break down. And as broke as I had been in college, I was now getting by with even less food money than when I lived in Winona.

To make a few extra bucks, I started selling plasma a couple times a week. The clinic was not in one of Minneapolis's better neighborhoods. Put it this way: My plasma money was going to food, but some of the other people there were more likely to take their $25 check next door and grab a few Olde English 800s.

I needed every dollar I could get. There were a couple of times where I'd be in the bathroom at the plasma donation center getting myself fired up, trying to get my blood pressure high enough to donate for the second time in a week. That was as often as they would let you donate. You got $25 the first time and then $35 the second time. So you could make $60 total, every week.

But there was a catch. If your blood pressure was too low, they couldn't take your plasma. And they would only check your pressure twice before they shut you down and sent you home. Sometimes, that put me in a bind. I'd be there in the bathroom, running in place, yelling at myself about how I needed that $35.

And if psyching myself up didn't do the trick, well, I was shit out of luck. I would miss out on the food money I needed for the weekend with no way to make more until Monday.

It became obvious pretty quickly that, for the first time in my life, I needed a real plan for my body. And that meant I needed to get an education about food.

I've met tons of people who tell me they want to fix their diet and get healthy, but they don't know where to start. And I can relate. It's a daunting task. There's just so much information out there. It's hard to make sense of it all.

But at that point, I desperately needed to figure things out.

When I started training, I weighed maybe 155 pounds, which is obviously not the size you associate with a pro wrestler. And I wasn't even necessarily a good 155 pounds. I was still 155 pounds of skinny fatness.

I was naturally really athletic, but I hadn't nurtured my body in any way for years. For several years leading up to that point, I had been partying a lot, and my nutritional intake still consisted solely of dumb convenient eating. I was still operating with very limited knowledge of diet and nutrition. I was really just winging it.

I hadn't learned much of anything about nutrition from my baseball coaches in high school or even college. And I'm not trying to bash those guys. They're not alone.

To this day, it's not uncommon to see stacks of pizza boxes backstage at a wrestling event. We're all oiled up and in Spandex trying to look our best in the ring. And now we're supposed to chow down on a couple slices of pepperoni pizza before we go out there and put on an athletic performance?

Terry Fox was certainly not going to school me in the ways of proper diet. Terry is a great wrestling instructor, but physically, he kind of resembles one of the Super Mario Brothers. His body was not exactly a temple.

So I got my information about training and diet the same way most guys do when they start out in wrestling. I went and bought some bodybuilding magazines. Or I'd hear guys talking in the locker room. And everyone more or less regurgitated the same message.

Eventually, you gather all the conventional wisdom, which sounds like this: Eat a lot of protein from animal sources—meat and eggs and whey protein shakes. (FYI—whey is one of the two proteins that make up milk. The other one is where cheese curds come from. You know, the Little Miss Muffet stuff.) Keep your fats down and eat mostly complex carbohydrates. There's lots of window dressing, but that's about it.

One way or another, I had gotten the message that the best way to get protein was from either chicken or fish. For me, fish was out. When I was four or five years old, my mom had given me some cheap, soggy, extra-fishy frozen fish sticks. And in one shot they completely ruined me on seafood. To this day, I can't stand the flavor or even the smell.

I never really ate a lot of pork. And at that point in my life, beef wasn't very cost-effective compared to my other options. So those two things kind of drifted away. (Crazy T would have been proud, wherever he was.)

Personally, I've never felt beholden to any particular food. I've never been the kind of person who would say, "I don't want to live if I can't eat steak" or anything like that. So for me, cutting out beef and pork wasn't much of a sacrifice.

That left chicken.

In my early days training to be a wrestler, I was eating a lot of chicken breasts and rice and broccoli and stuff like that. I was also eating a lot of eggs.

(Milk, though, was off the list. I never liked milk, even as a kid. I could deal with it in cereal. And I liked the occasional chocolate milk. But otherwise, milk was always weird and disgusting to me.)

But then one day, in late 2000, less than a year after I had committed myself to wrestling, I bought my bag of chicken breasts intending to cook them up and store them in the fridge. This was part of my weekly routine. I was loading myself up on protein, just like everyone had told me to.

I remember I had the bag thawed out, and I started cooking one of the breasts. But somehow, it just didn't look very appetizing.

Actually, it was more than that. It looked really gross.

I tried to ignore it. I needed to eat this chicken, I thought. I needed the protein.

But I couldn't do it. The idea of eating chicken seemed really offensive to me, plain and simple. Eating another living creature was just no longer appetizing.

That may sound weird to meat eaters, but let me put it this way: If that had been dog meat, you'd probably agree with me. If it was giraffe meat, that might seem pretty off-putting to you, too. Well, in that moment—and ever since—I just couldn't see what made a chicken any different.

It wasn't about flavor. I had been raised eating chicken. I had acquired the taste, just like everybody else.

I have the same childhood memories as you probably do: The McDonald's we used to go to near my grandma and grandpa's house. Those KFC drumsticks I used to wash down with Mountain Dew as a kid.

When I was younger, I looked forward to Thanksgiving just like everyone else did. But now, all I could think about was a headless bird corpse sitting in the middle of my table and how I'm supposed to be excited to rip its leg off and then grab some stuffing out of its asshole.

Over the years, a whole bunch of seeds had been planted in my head, and now, suddenly, they were all starting to come together and take root. I could no longer ignore all the things I had experienced: My Grandpa Manny's cows. That slaughterhouse Crazy T and I had driven past in Texas.

Since I had gotten out on my own, I'd had so many experiences and met so many people who had challenged my notions of how life worked. I had spent a lot of long hours trying to figure out who I was and what I believed in.

More and more, I had started to think about my place in the world. How did I feel about participating in a system that caused the unnecessary and brutal death of millions of animals? Did

I feel comfortable knowing that a life had to be taken just so I could have something to eat?

I could no longer pretend I didn't know what I was eating or where it had come from. I couldn't pretend it didn't bother me. I couldn't put my head back in the sand. I couldn't disconnect the dots.

That was the last time I deliberately ate meat.

And truthfully, I've never missed it.

CHAPTER 3

If it wasn't for wrestling, I don't know if I would have ever stopped eating animals. It's definitely possible I'd still be eating meat today.

When I was younger, sure, I might have felt weird about reeling in a fish, or had second thoughts about eating cows at my Grandpa Manny's farm. But I don't think it's all that unusual to have those reactions. From time to time, I think a lot of people feel squeamish about eating animals, at least a little bit. But we tend to ignore those feelings because our culture promotes the idea that meat eating is a natural, everyday activity. The world tells us to suppress those reactions, and to tune them out.

The world also programs us to think that we should feel comfortable eating certain animals, but weird about eating other ones. If it's a cow or a pig, we're told that's cool. But change C-O-W to D-O-G or P-I-G to C-A-T, and now we're told that's disgusting. When you break it down, there's no real rhyme or reason for the distinctions we make among the animals we keep as pets and the animals we kill for food. But when you hear that stuff early and often, you accept those distinctions as "normal."

So who knows? Maybe I could have gone on ignoring how weird I felt about being a carnivore. I might have told myself the same things a lot of people tell themselves (whether they really believe them or not): I'm the top of the food chain. I'm a savage beast. Give me a steak, extra bloody, and skip the fork—I'll eat it with my bare hands.

There are all kinds of justifications for eating meat to fall back on if you really want to find one. I'm sure everyone has heard the theory that humans are supposed to be carnivorous because of our canine teeth, right? That's usually one of the go-to defenses against a plant-based diet.

Well, let's talk about that a little bit: Yes, they may be called canines. But if you really look at the teeth, they are not all that sharp. They're actually pretty blunt, when you compare them to the teeth of other carnivores, like dogs. They're not really ideal for ripping flesh. Also, chimpanzees have some pretty fierce teeth, and they're basically just plant eaters. And don't forget, meat isn't the only food that's hard to chew. The same also goes for nuts, for example. Or how about this: Maybe we have sharp teeth for self-defense purposes?

Maybe, just maybe, the shape of our teeth doesn't tell the whole truth about what our diet should be.

When you actually do a little homework, the canine teeth argument for eating meat really doesn't hold a lot of water. As I've found, neither do a lot of the arguments for eating animals.

But most people don't bother to do a little digging and find some real facts. Because they're not interested in facts. They're not interested in truth. They just want to hear some kind of justification that defends the status quo. Really, they just assume that eating meat is what they're supposed to do because that's the way they've been raised. They don't ever give the subject much thought.

Life is a never-ending series of choices. I could've made some different decisions along the way that might have steered my life in another direction. If I had met some different people, or gone some different places, or had some different jobs, it's possible I might have had a completely different career and developed a whole different mindset.

If my life had turned out differently, I might well have made the choice to stay ignorant. The system would definitely prefer that you do. The world makes it really easy for you to stay the course and keep eating what you're told. And that doesn't just apply to meat. That also applies to the thousands of barely-edible products we see every day in supermarkets and on TV commercials.

But when wrestling found me, it forced me to start taking a serious look at health and diet. Wrestling led me down a path which opened my mind about the food I eat.

I believe that everything happens for a reason. Looking back, there were a string of events that led me to where I am today. Working at that pizza place in Winona put me in contact with my friend Steve. Steve's interstate weed operation introduced me to Crazy T, who then planted the seed in my mind about not eating beef and pork. Getting that phone call from Justin introduced me to wrestling. If I had made it to Lake Havasu before Justin hit me up, instead of when I was back in Minnesota, would I have dropped everything to go check out a wrestling school? I doubt it. The pieces all tie together.

I believe it was my destiny to become a pro wrestler. And wrestling made me take a long hard look at the food I'd been raised eating.

So who knows? In a roundabout way, maybe I was destined to become a vegan as well.

During those first few years as a wrestler, I was working very hard at the gym and even harder training in the ring. And that had some trickle-down effects. Like a lot of people who get really into fitness, I wasn't going to throw away all that hard work consuming a bunch of empty calories.

Soda was one of the first things to go. Growing up, I drank generic Mountain Dew all the time. And then I continued drinking soda through college. It wasn't necessarily something I bought at the store. Out at the bars, though, I always had my rum and Cokes or vodka 7-Ups. But once I started wrestling, soda didn't fit into my diet, and it didn't fit into my budget either. I also cut out juice and iced tea and things like that. I needed to eliminate anything that cost money and didn't give me a high nutritional value, so dropping those was a no-brainer. To this day, I might enjoy a good ginger beer here or there, but that was pretty much the end of sugary drinks for me.

For a while there, when I first started training, alcohol was all but eliminated from my life. I might still smoke a little bit of weed at night to help me relax and recover. But I never smoked before training. I always wanted to be 100% in the ring. I always wanted to have a clear head. I had the mindset of an athlete again, like back when I'd played baseball.

At this point, I don't really need to defend marijuana anymore, do I? Unlike alcohol or pain pills, it's never killed anyone. At the end of some long, grueling days, I found it really helped my pain management.

And as someone who was trying to put size on, it was also a really good appetite stimulator. I was trying to eat six times a day, which did not come naturally to me, so I would work my smoke sessions around meal times.

I also felt like bud helped me get the creative juices flowing. It helped me come up with my moves and my name. From the first day I trained, I kept a notebook. At night, I'd write down pages and pages of notes on moves I wanted to try and ideas for my character.

I have to give marijuana at least partial credit for some of the gimmicks I came up with. One of them, Frank Zeno, "Fucking Rock Star," is pretty self-explanatory. I used that name later for Zeno's Revenge, a shitty cover band I sang in with some college buddies.

And then there was Dan "Casual" Sexon. I put on a fake moustache and covered up my tattoo to "hide" my Austin Aries persona, then I put on a leisure suit and teamed up with my buddy Brody Hoofer, who called himself "The Piston" Ted Dixon.

Together, we were The Dixon-Sexon Connexion.

We came out to Curtis Mayfield's "Get Down," complete with hip thrusting and head shaking, and we refused to ever admit that we were really Aries and Hoofer. I had an overly-endowed package, enhanced by a sock stuffed full of socks, and occasionally a foreign object (like a cue ball) that came in handy for cold-cocking an opponent when a ref wasn't looking. (Pun obviously intended.)

Marijuana definitely helped me come up with some of the moves I use to this day. I would sit there with my notebook and I would think, well, Tajiri did a front handspring into a back elbow. I don't want to do exactly the same thing he does, but that's kind of a cool idea. So I can do that front handspring and jump back into a DDT. Or I can do a front handspring and jump into a moonsault.

That became part of my weekly routine. I would write a bunch of stuff out at night, and then the next day I would go try it at camp. Some stuff would work out, and naturally some stuff wouldn't. But a lot of the moves that worked became my staples, like the running dropkick in the corner. It's a simple thing. I figured, hey, nobody ever does that when they're running at a guy who's standing in a corner. Everybody just runs in and does the elbow.

Over time, as I perfected my dropkick, it became an important part of my move set. Now it's one of the things that I'll hit a guy with leading into my finish, "The Brainbuster," which was a move I always liked seeing back in the day. Dick Murdoch and Jimmy Garvin both did "The Brainbuster," as did one of my favorites, "Double A" Arn Anderson. Eddie Guerrero also had a sweet Brainbuster later on, too.

That was my go-to creative process. You smoke a little bit, and then you just start letting the ideas flow. Thank you, sweet Mary Jane.

Once I swore off eating meat, I had to figure out how I was

going to get enough protein. I was vaguely aware that there were some vegetarian options available at the grocery store. So at first, instead of buying my chicken breasts, I just started buying the closest vegetarian equivalents. I could eat a veggie burger or some veggie chicken nuggets, and by the time I added condiments, I could barely tell the difference.

For a while there after going vegetarian, that was all that really changed in my life. MorningStar Farms veggie hot dogs had about ten grams of protein each, so I ate tons of those. Plus, I was still eating eggs and dairy and whey protein. The transition wasn't all that hard.

Around that time, my cooking skills began to improve. As a broke college kid, I had mostly learned to cook out of necessity. But now that I had put restrictions on what I would and would not eat, I had to get a little more creative.

For breakfast, I started taking potatoes and onions and then throwing in some 99-cent frozen black bean chili plus maybe a veggie breakfast sausage. I'd add some salsa and cheese, and boom—that was my breakfast concoction for a long time.

Until I started reading labels to make sure I didn't accidentally eat meat, I never would have thought a frozen entrée of rice and beans could somehow contain two paragraphs' worth of ingredients. That might have been the start of me getting weird about eating products that included a laundry list of mystery additives.

I couldn't identify half the stuff they put in frozen rice and beans. I don't think many normal people can. It seemed easier to me to just cook up some rice and some beans by myself. That way, I knew there were just two ingredients: rice and beans. Doing that was more time consuming, but it was also cheaper.

I also realized that if I was trying to eat healthy, nutritious foods, I shouldn't use a microwave all the time. Studies suggest that microwaves can alter nutrients in food, amongst other adverse effects. I mean, I like convenience as much as anybody else. I still own a microwave, and I'll use it if I'm feeling lazy or

I'm really crunched for time. But on a day-to-day basis, I figured why not just take the extra five minutes and heat up my food on the stovetop?

Let me be clear: Even though I had made the decision to stop eating meat, that doesn't mean I was instantly well-educated about nutrition. I was still eating at Taco Bell all the time. And obviously, just because your Taco Bell burrito doesn't include meat, that does not make it health food by any stretch of the imagination. I would just get a bean and rice burrito or maybe a seven-layer.

All these years later, I look back and laugh at my Taco Bell love fest. Nowadays, I'd have to be beyond starving to consume that shit.

Luckily, in another nice little twist of fate, during those first few years I was wrestling, I lucked out and found the best regular job I ever had, working as a lunch server in a small Kurdish restaurant called Babani's. The owner was this incredibly nice guy named Rodwan Nakshabandi. Rodwan and his family are some of the sweetest, most hardworking people I've ever come across.

A lot of people might tell you the American dream is dead, but to someone like Rodwan, the American dream is absolutely alive and well. He came over from Kurdistan to get away from all the Saddam Hussein craziness. He eventually brought over his wife Sepal and her sister Maha, too. He was able to open his business, raise a family, and be successful doing something he loves alongside the people he loves.

To people who've never tried eating vegetarian, a diet with no meat might seem kind of limited. But in reality, putting restrictions on what I would and wouldn't eat made me open my mind to a bunch of foods I probably never would have tried. Before I met Rodwan and his family, I had never eaten lentils. I think I'd heard of hummus, but I had never tried it. Those quickly became two of my favorite foods.

I had worked in restaurants before, but they had usually been more of the greasy spoon variety. Back in Winona, during my college days, I waited tables at a place called Betty Jo Belowski's. A typical work meal there would have been a sloppy joe loaded up with mystery meat, or something else that really wasn't doing much good for anyone's body.

Right before I started waiting tables at Babani's, I also worked at a Houlihan's. Even though I had stopped eating meat a few months earlier, one day I found myself getting really tempted by one of the Houlihan's Buffalo chicken salads.

To this day, I love Buffalo sauce. Nowadays, I can whip you up some Buffalo cauliflower and I promise you will not care one bit that you're eating vegetables instead of meat.

But that day, in the middle of a long double shift, I said fuck it and went for the chicken salad. Well, that salad might have looked good, and it might have smelled good, but I got two bites in and gave up. I just couldn't do it. That was the last temptation. I haven't eaten meat since, at least on purpose.

Eating at Babani's was a complete 180 from my experience with that Houlihan's chicken salad. Once I started waiting tables for Rodwan, every weekday at 3 o'clock, after lunch service, I'd sit down with him and his family and we'd all eat together. There would always be garbanzo beans, rice, vegetables and this amazing Kurdish bread with a spicy red sauce.

The restaurant is still there, in downtown St. Paul. I try to go there every time I'm back in Minnesota. And every time I walk in, they treat me like I never left.

In fact, let me give them a plug right now. Next time you're in the Twin Cities area, check out Babani's Kurdish Restaurant, located at 544 St. Peter Street in St. Paul, or find them on the web at Babanis.com. And tell them I sent you.

For a vegetarian bachelor with very little money, finding that job was an amazing score. My diet improved immensely just by working there. And more importantly, I didn't have to work on weekends, so I was free to go off and wrestle whenever I could.

I had my first wrestling match at the end of 2000—almost the exact same time I stopped eating meat. It was your typical independent wrestling show. There was a very minimal setup. There was a ring, some chairs, a lot of hopes and dreams, and not a whole lot of paying customers. There might have been 150 people there, all told. But after all that training and dietary discipline, it was exciting to finally get out in front of people and perform.

The match was held at the Bloomington Armory in Minnesota. It went pretty well considering how god awful my opponent was. He was supposed to be an experienced veteran, but the guy couldn't remember a god damn thing.

I may have given him a concussion, which probably didn't help. Early on, I did a front flip leg drop and I landed on his head a little bit. He was loopy after that. I had to carry him along, moving him through all his stuff the rest of the way, in my first match.

When you wrestle at the independent level, you do a lot more than just show up and body slam dudes. You help set up the ring before the doors open, and then after everyone goes home, you break it back down. But I didn't care. No job was too small, as long as I got some ring time. I definitely had the bug.

My second match I wrestled a huge jacked up 230-pound dude named "The Black Stallion." The ref for that match was a 15-year-old Shawn Daivari, all 145 pounds of him, who appeared under the name Oliver Clotheshoff.

I wrestled as often as I could, which was usually a couple times a month. A guy named "Sheriff" Johnny Emeril ran a little promotion called Minnesota Independent Wrestling. Sometimes there would be wrestling at an outdoor festival somewhere. Early on, I worked a lot of Terry Fox and Eddie Sharkey's shows. Eddie would run a show in a bar every once in a while.

Terry would run a show every month or so. He was good

to us. He'd always pay us something at the end of the night. I remember, after one of those Dixon-Sexon Connexion tag team appearances, Terry handed me $23. Then he gave my partner "The Piston" $17. To this day, I have no idea why. I told Brody that maybe I was just six bucks better than him that night.

I spent the next four years honing my skills and getting more experience, first working at local shows, then branching out from Minnesota and picking up bookings in Milwaukee, Chicago, and beyond.

The first time I ventured out of Minneapolis, I drove all the way to Iowa. A guy I knew from Minnesota named "Playboy" Pete Huge invited me to tag along for an open slot at a show he was doing. It might have been my tenth match ever.

It turned out to be a tables, ladders, and chairs match. That was the night I learned that you can't jump off a ladder unless someone is holding the damn thing. Because the minute you take off, the ladder is the thing that goes flying. You just fall straight down.

I landed on the table chin-fist. I almost decapitated myself.

To give you an idea of the caliber of this event, the table wasn't even a table. It was a door that had legs screwed into it. As it was explained to me, tables cost about $30. But the cheapest doors you could buy were $7.99. So they would buy a door and screw some legs in, and then whenever the door broke, they'd unscrew the legs and then screw them into the next $7.99 door.

I think I got paid $30—or the cost of one actual table—to drive all that way and almost take my own head off. Those were the glory days right there.

The more I wrestled, the more I was able to define my style. Growing up, I had gravitated toward the smaller, more athletic wrestlers. Now that I was stepping into the ring as an undersized guy myself, I spent a lot of those early formative years trying to figure out how a guy like me could realistically go toe-to-toe with dudes who were much bigger than me.

The way I looked at it, pro wrestlers are like action heroes. And every action hero has a skillset. So I tried to figure out what super powers I could have that would be different and special enough to match up against other superheroes and their own set of super powers.

I learned to lean on my quickness and speed and my athleticism coming off the ropes. I also worked hard on becoming technically sound with my ground game. Because no matter how big a guy is, if you can get him on the mat, you can submit him.

Around that time, as the internet started getting bigger, a local journalist and wrestling fan named Tim Larson created a monthly online newsletter. Tim was the first guy to get the names of independent wrestlers in the Midwest like me out there to wrestling fans everywhere else.

Tim was also responsible for introducing me to a guy I'm still very close with to this day. Angel Armani was probably in his mid-40s when we met. But unlike a lot of the other older guys I encountered, Angel took me under his wing and really tried to help me.

When I got started, wrestling was changing. Up-and-comers like me were doing lots of high-energy, high-impact moves. A lot of the old guys would complain, because we'd do all our crazy stuff on the undercard and then they'd have to follow us in the main event.

I can understand why those guys got a little salty. We were probably doing bigger stuff than we needed to be doing that early in the show. But instead of recognizing how hungry we were, and taking some time to sit down with us to try to teach us how to harness our potential more effectively, a lot of the old guys would just bitch at us instead.

Angel was the first experienced guy who didn't do that. We ended up becoming really tight. We were even roommates for about six months. He gave me a place to stay back in Milwaukee when I needed one.

Before I moved down there and roomed with him, Armani and I had a phone conversation that has stuck with me to this day. We were talking about how much dedication it takes to make it in wrestling. It's not a very sensible career path when you think about it. You really have to love it, to the point of insanity.

It was a Friday. And out of nowhere, Armani asked me if I wanted $100 bucks. I told him I would like that very much.

"Then here's what I'm going to do," he said. "I'm going to go outside right now, and I'm going to nail a $100 bill to a tree in my backyard. Come and get it. It's yours."

I was in Minneapolis at the time. I reminded him that, as much as I could use the money, he was about a five-hour drive away. That was a long way to go for $100.

"Okay," he said, and then our conversation continued.

"Hey, I'm running a show on Saturday," he added, a bit later. "I can pay you $100. Can you do it?"

That's when I got it.

"Fuck you," I said with a laugh.

He had made his point. No, I wouldn't drive ten hours round trip to get a free $100. But of course I would make that drive if I had a chance to get in the ring and beat myself up.

Once I moved back down to Milwaukee, I took part in Angel's show all the time. That show allowed me to branch out of the Minnesota area, and it also led to me wrestling for Ian Rotten and IWA Mid-South. Ian had a lot of name guys wrestling for him, and a lot of buzz, too. Wrestling for IWA Mid-South gave me the opportunity to meet some even bigger guys and bigger wrestling promotions. It also got me in the door at the first show I ever did in Kentucky.

Ken Anderson and I drove straight through for 15 or 16 hours, all the way from Minneapolis to Louisville. We weren't getting paid much, just gas money plus a few bucks to wrestle. But that wasn't the point. This was a big opportunity for both of us. We were really excited the whole way down.

Our mood went south pretty quickly. After that long drive, we weren't exactly welcomed with open arms. There were a lot of different guys there from a lot of different parts of the country, and I think some regional clique-type bullshit came into play.

Ken got sent to one locker room and I got sent to another. And then, as the event got underway, I just sat there and waited. The show went on for five long hours, which I spent more or less in silence alongside a bunch of old dudes I didn't know who made it clear they weren't interested in striking up a friendship.

I remember there was a shower stall and a bench in that locker room, but no toilet. Instead, there was a bucket, which slowly filled up with everyone's piss as the night dragged on.

Finally, Ken and I got our chance. CM Punk was doing commentary that night. Being the nice guy he is, he proceeded to bury us.

I can't really say I blame him. Ken and I were not on our game. Maybe it was nerves. Maybe it was that long car ride. Maybe it was the warm welcome we had received. Maybe we just sucked. We had the best of intentions, but we just didn't click that night.

At the end of the show, despite our earlier financial arrangement, Ian Rotten gave us a choice between getting paid for wrestling or getting gas money, but not both. Obviously, no matter which option we chose, that just meant we were piling back in the car, driving another 15 hours, and going home empty-handed—minus the Taco Bell we grabbed on the ride back, of course.

But that's the way it was. You took any work you could get. Sometimes, at the end of the night you didn't have much to show for your efforts. But you gained more experience, got some exposure, and made some new connections.

I was just trying to keep the ball rolling, so I took every road trip opportunity that came my way. One catalyst to my growth was when Shawn Daivari and I drove down to Tennessee to a camp put together by "Dr. Tom" Prichard, who was Head of Talent Relations for the WWE at the time. During that trip I also tagged along when Daivari had a dark match at TNA.

A dark match is a match that happens before a pay-per-view goes live, or before the cameras start rolling for a TV taping. The purpose of dark matches is to warm the crowd up a little bit and to check the cameras and the sound equipment before the marquee action begins.

Promoters sometimes use dark matches as trial matches, to see how a guy performs in front of a crowd. I must have made a decent impression on some people when I came along with Daivari for his dark match, because that led to my own tryout match against the former Crash Holly, who was now wrestling in TNA as Mad Mikey.

Most importantly, I was able to turn my performance at Dr. Tom's camp into a couple of WWE dark matches, too. My first one was actually against Shawn Daivari. Then we teamed up to take on the famed table-breaking Dudley Boys. Years later, I found out the Dudleys had gotten forced into a dark match against a couple of "local greenhorn no-names" as a form of punishment.

WWE decided that although I showed potential, I didn't fit the mold they were looking for at the time. Regardless, it was a great experience and it was still a step in the right direction. I was as motivated as ever.

Thanks to those dark matches, some buzz was beginning to generate. I got invited to the Super 8 Tournament, which is historically one of the more well-known indie tournaments. After a good showing and making it to the finals of Super 8, I got some coverage in *Pro Wrestling Illustrated* magazine, one of the magazines I used to read as kid in the magazine section at Walmart while my mom did our family's shopping.

By this point, I guess I'd improved a bit since that match with Ken Anderson in Kentucky, because right around that time, CM Punk helped put me in touch with Ring of Honor's Gabe Sapolsky. I hopped in a van full of other dudes and headed out to New Jersey for what's known as a Do-or-Die Match. The name is pretty self-explanatory. They throw you out in front of a crowd, and the crowd decides if they like you or not.

New Jersey was a tough crowd, but I managed to win them over…by doing every cool move I could think of. I didn't know any better at the time, but in that instance it worked. Ring of Honor decided they liked me and wanted to start using me. So I decided to make it easy for them and go where the action was. In 2004, I packed up my stuff and moved to Philadelphia.

As I made my way through the national wrestling community as a vegetarian, of course there was some good-natured ballbusting. But it was all in good fun. That just goes with the territory. Most people were curious more than anything else. Most high-level athletes travel with supplements, or follow some sort of unusual or extreme diet. In my circle, everyone was a weirdo in their own way. I was just the one who didn't eat meat.

I've never wanted to make people feel like they have to go out of their way to accommodate my diet. I always try to make sure I'm not a stick in the mud. If everyone wanted to go out to a steakhouse after a wrestling show, I'd go, too. But when they ordered their steaks, I'd get a spinach salad. I started carrying these packs of pre-cooked black lentils around with me, and when I added my lentils to the salad, I was getting over 45 grams of protein.

Likewise, the couple of times a year I made it back to see my family, I always made sure I brought food with me. If my family was going to eat some chicken, I'd bring my meatless chicken nuggets and make those instead. If they wanted to grill out, I'd bring Tofurkey sausages or veggie burgers, so I could still eat with everyone else and be a part of the gathering. It's not as difficult as some people make it out to be.

As my wrestling career progressed, so did my education about food. I took greater and greater ownership of my diet. Long gone were the days when I could eat whatever was easy and right in front of me. Food was now a priority in a way it had never been before.

I was used to shopping for food on a limited budget. But now I needed to get the most possible nutritional bang for my buck. Back in my college days, I used to load up on 89-cent hot dogs and those 3-for-1 mac and cheeses. Now, I was more concerned with figuring out how to get the most protein and quality nutrients for my dollar.

I would look at loaves of bread, read the backs of the labels, and do some math. Okay, I'd think, these two loaves both contain 20 slices of bread. Only this one has 3 grams of protein a slice, and this one has 5 grams of protein a slice. So if they're both the same price, then I'm going with the one with more protein.

Lance Storm has said that when he eats, he's not thinking about what he wants to eat. He's thinking strictly about how he can make his body perform at the highest level possible. He looks at food purely as fuel.

Once wrestling became the sole focus of my life, I started looking at food the same way. It was almost like a game I was playing with myself. I had certain priorities. I had the numbers I needed to hit every day in terms of protein and fat and so on.

When I was at the grocery store, the foods that didn't help me hit those numbers got cut. I used to eat cereal sometimes for breakfast, but pretty soon that got nixed, because in terms of nutrition, cereal didn't give me what I needed from my food.

Looking back, even with as much progress as I had made by then, I still had a long way to go. I tried to be healthy and fit, but when I first moved to Philly, I remember settling on an apartment because it was near my gym, my bank, and yes, you guessed it: Taco Bell. I remember thinking it would be really handy to live near all three of those places. That shows you where my priorities were, even several years after I became a vegetarian.

Even so, the more I saw results for my efforts, the more my interest in the food I was eating kept expanding. Every piece of information I learned opened a door to things that I didn't know. So I kept upping the ante, so to speak.

I wanted to know everything. And not just about vegetarianism.

As I read up on diet and fitness, it wasn't long before I started to come across some pretty disturbing stuff about fake sugar. As a society, I think lots of people have developed a healthy skepticism about sugar replacements. I was really just riding that wave.

I read about studies that have been done on sucralose, which is the scientific name for Splenda. They put Splenda in products so they can call them sugar-free and so people think the product's better for them.

But it's not that simple. There's lots of evidence that suggests that fake sugar is not any less fattening for you than plain old sugar is. In terms of overall health, it might actually be worse, when you factor in the potential side effects.

Look, the people who make fake sugar can claim whatever they want. But tell me something: If you wake up tomorrow and go on the internet and all of a sudden the scientific community is saying, "Whoops, fake sugar is just as fattening as real sugar," or "Whoops, it turns out this stuff is giving us all cancer," could anybody really be surprised? I sure as hell wouldn't. That's pretty much exactly what happened with cigarettes.

If it's bad for lab rats, I figured it's probably not good for anything with a pulse, including me. So at that point, I decided I was done with artificial sweeteners.

I think the next subject I did a real deep dive on was organic food. "Organic" has become such a big buzzword over the last few years. But I wanted to understand the real differences between organic and non-organic.

If you don't already know, organic means fruits and vegetables that have been grown without the use of pesticides or synthetic fertilizers and without any genetic modifications. To put it as simply as possible, by eating organic foods, you reduce the amount of toxins you're consuming. I think most people would agree that if you can reduce the amount of man-made chemicals you're eating and drinking, over the long haul that will probably be beneficial to your health. It's really just that straightforward.

Once I learned what eating organic food meant, I decided to try to eat organic as often as possible. I know sometimes the organic movement is associated with wacky crunchy granola types and annoying Gwyneth Paltrow-style yuppies. But if not wanting to eat chemicals makes me a hippy or a yuppie, well, then, I guess that's what I am.

Once I started buying organic produce, I made an interesting discovery: It tastes better. Organic bananas taste better. Organic apples taste better. They just do. They taste more like the fruits and vegetables you remember eating as a kid.

And then there's another thing I don't think most people realize: Organic produce seems to keep two or three times longer. I've kept apples in my fridge for months with no problems. When I buy organic bananas, they don't ripen and spoil within two or three days like regular bananas do.

Think about that the next time you're at the grocery store. Sure, the organic stuff is more expensive. But are you just going to end up throwing the other stuff in the garbage when it goes bad in a couple days?

As long as we're on the subject, let me throw a little conspiracy theory out there: I've come to wonder if the people who grow and sell non-organic fruits and vegetables actually want their stuff to go bad faster so you have to go buy more. Think about it. They've been able to use chemicals and genetic modifications to make all these things grow bigger and be resistant to pests, but somehow they can't stop them from spoiling so fast? I'm calling bullshit.

Over my first few years in wrestling, since I was trying to sculpt my body, for the first time in my life I started getting a handle on what portion sizes are supposed to look like and what kind of caloric intake I should be shooting for. I quickly realized that the average portion of pasta most people eat, for example, contains far more carbohydrates than most people are supposed to eat in one sitting. And believe it or not, I discovered that a double cheeseburger contains more meat and cheese than most humans are really supposed to eat at one time, too. I know—who would have guessed?

As it turns out, one practical skill came out of my drug running days. I became really good at numbers and scales, which came in handy when I started measuring all of my food out.

When people ask me for advice about changing their diet, I always tell them to start with buying a food scale and keeping a food diary. If you read the nutritional information on a box of food, they always tell you what a portion size is supposed to be. But most people don't bother to read that, and even fewer people ever bother to weigh that out.

We've been programmed by society to eat way more than we should be eating. As I started really getting into shape, for the first time in my life, that reality was staring me in the face in cold hard numbers. The first time I weighed out a portion of pasta, I was blown away. Without a scale, I would have eaten three times the portion size you're really supposed to have.

No one teaches us to stop eating when we've had a proper serving, because the people who sell us food make more money when we stuff ourselves. They tell us that bigger is better and encourage an all-you-can-eat mentality. (You're definitely never going to see an all-you-*should*-eat restaurant.)

A couple of years after I cut fake sugars out of my diet, all the stuff I was learning about portion sizes made me started paying more attention to real sugar, too.

Even if you bother to check the sugar levels on labels, to most people they're really just a bunch of meaningless numbers. I certainly wasn't equipped with any sort of mental measuring stick. So I began to wonder how many grams of sugar you can consume before it becomes really unhealthy.

A 12-ounce can of soda might contain 35 grams of sugar. To put it in perspective, that's almost ten teaspoons.

Think about that. If you watched your friend shovel 10 teaspoons of sugar in his coffee, you would probably tackle him to make him stop. And what if you saw him do it at breakfast, and then again at lunch, and then again at dinner? You'd probably stage an intervention. But that's the reality of sugar intake for tons and tons of people.

When I was a kid, it was no big deal for me to drink two or three cans of soda in a day. Some people drink way more than that. And people wonder why we have an obesity epidemic?

In December of 2004, after I relocated to Philadelphia, I shockingly took the Ring of Honor title off of Samoa Joe. Joe had held the belt for almost two years. It was an amazing run. I had a huge amount of respect for Joe and what he'd accomplished. It was a pretty big act to follow.

I knew I was unlikely to compete with the length of his title run, so I decided to try and put my own stamp on the title by attempting to make it a true world title. I defended the belt internationally as often as I could. I did Austria, Switzerland, Canada, and then Mexico.

That was the first time I ever went to Mexico. As a vegetarian, it was an eye-opening experience to say the least. I remember walking around some little town south of Mexico City, looking for some lunch, and seeing a bunch of butcher shops with all of these dead animals hanging everywhere. It was really in your face.

That made me think of people in America who go around saying things like, "I could never give up bacon." If some of those people had to walk down the street every day looking at dead, gutted pigs hanging in store windows, I wonder if some of them might change their tune. Come sit next to a dead pig and eat some bacon, and then tell me that's something you can't live without. It's a whole different ballgame when it's out in the open like that. But our culture encourages people to stick their heads in the sand and to ignore the reality of eating meat.

About six months later, I lost the belt, but shortly after that I started running Ring of Honor's training school. Although my work at that school was obviously outside the public eye, between my world title reign and then holding that job title, I really cemented a name for myself in the industry.

I enjoyed training guys. It was a lot of fun. And I'd like to think I was pretty good at it. When I was coming up, my training had been rooted in really solid fundamentals. At the Ring of Honor school, I tried to set a high standard and to pass those fundamentals on to some other guys.

I have always found that if you do the work and show the industry the respect it deserves, the industry will recognize that and respect you back. And if you go about your business the right way, this industry can provide some pretty amazing opportunities.

At that point, for the first time in my career, wrestling really started paying the bills and providing me with a comfortable lifestyle. I was working full-time on a national stage, and I was able to command good paydays from the indies on the side.

I remember when I first signed that waiver for Terry Fox and committed to paying him $3000 to train me. At that time in my life, right after I dropped out of college, $3000 was a shitload of money. Back when I was making 20 bucks a match and wrestling maybe twice a month, I remember crunching the numbers and figuring out that at that rate it was going to take me a long, long time to recoup my initial investment. I wasn't sure I would ever get over that hump, much less be able to support myself without waiting tables on the side.

And now I was able to go out, wrestle a couple shows, and make that kind of money in a weekend. Obviously I wasn't a millionaire. But that's when I felt like I'd accomplished my initial goal. I felt like I'd really made it.

Some guys finish college and walk straight into a development deal. Or they go right from a failed NFL career to a full-time wrestling gig. They never have to set up a ring or drive 12 hours to wrestle and make 30 bucks for their efforts. But I'm proud of the journey I took. I wouldn't trade it for an easier route. Every time the curtain opens and I walk out, I bring that journey with me. That's the mentality that I have. It's what drives me to be the greatest every time out.

I ran the ROH school for a couple years. By the time I was done there, I'd also started wrestling for TNA, in addition to Ring of Honor.

My first go-round with TNA was a little rocky. The atmosphere behind the scenes was a little more corporate, shall we say, than what I was used to. I quickly found out that certain performers weren't supposed to ask questions. We were just supposed to shut up and perform. There were also politics there that affected my outside bookings, including ROH, and that was hurting my income.

It reminded me of the culture I grew up in back in Waukesha. Things are the way they are and everyone is just supposed go along with it. It's the same deal with the food we're all raised eating. You're supposed to eat cows, pigs, and chickens, and you're supposed to eat whatever processed garbage that corporations put on your plate. And somehow, if anyone doesn't go along with the program, that makes them a weirdo or a troublemaker.

I don't function well in that kind of atmosphere. If something strikes me as odd or flat-out wrong, I start asking questions. And—at least my first time around at TNA—I found out that my questions weren't welcome. They wanted "Yes, sir" while I preferred "Why, sir?"

I soon left TNA, which allowed me to return to ROH full-time. After a short time there, I adopted a flashier persona, almost in direct contrast to the "wrestling machine" I'd been. I began touting myself as "The Greatest Man That Ever Lived." I was all braggadocio, but I could back it up in the ring. The people hated it, and that was the point. In 2009, I became the first ever two-time Ring of Honor World Champion.

By 2010, I decided to move back to Milwaukee. I was getting flown to wherever the events were held, so I didn't really need to be in Philadelphia anymore. And I had never really embraced living in Philly. I've got nothing against that place. It just wasn't for me, at least at that point in my life.

Unfortunately, I didn't find whatever I was looking for in Milwaukee, and so from there I headed back to Minneapolis. I came to realize that, whatever my issue was, it was bigger than which city I chose to live in. The real truth was this: I had given wrestling my full commitment, and now, after ten years, I felt like I was spinning my wheels.

I needed a break. I wouldn't say that I almost retired. I certainly didn't make any public announcement. I always knew I'd find my way back to the ring. I just needed to take a step back and try something different, to recharge my batteries a bit.

By now, my buddy Justin was living in Los Angeles. And once again, just like when I joined him at Terry Fox and Eddie Sharkey's wrestling school, ten years earlier, I found myself heading his way. I ultimately spent a month in L.A., chilling with Justin and trying to figure out what my next move was going to be.

Unlike anywhere else I've lived before or since, Los Angeles is a mecca for vegetarians and vegans. Not only are there tons of restaurants and grocery stores for people who are meat-free, in Southern California there are just a lot more people who embrace a meatless lifestyle, at least compared to what I found in Philly and the Midwest.

Being in that environment instantly stimulated my desire to learn more about food and to dive deeper into the why's and how's of a wholesome healthy diet. For the first time in many years, a full week went by with no wrestling bookings on my schedule.

I worked towards getting certified as a personal trainer. I

also decided to enroll in a plant-based culinary school. I was just about to put pen to paper to make that official when I got a call from TNA. They were putting together an X Division Showcase.

"You want to come down for this match?" they asked.

I figured it couldn't hurt. Plus, I could use the payday. Once there, I made some amends and mended some fences. I was asked back for a second match. The winner of that match would receive a contract. I won, and then just like that, as quickly as I had gotten out, I was right back in.

Although I never made it to that culinary school, that didn't mean my food education had ended. On the contrary, once social media really took off, my attitudes toward food started evolving even more quickly. You can't be a vegetarian and a pro wrestler and not start running into some like-minded individuals. Through the connections and relationships I had made, I discovered an online community of people who were thinking about food along the same lines that I was.

Some of them were vegetarian. Some ate meat, but were just very conscious about the food they chose to eat. Everyone was doing what they were doing for their own personal reasons and in their own personal way. But there were common threads that tied us all together.

You start interacting with these people, and you start seeing things that people post. There are informational links or recommendations for documentaries to check out. As you learn more, you start peeling back more and more layers of information. It strengthens your reasons for believing what you believe and encourages you to question even more.

I started going further and further down a wormhole. More and more, I saw that a lot of what we eat comes down to what "they" tell us to eat. But that raises the question: Who are "they"?

For starters, take the almighty food pyramid. Even if most people couldn't name everything on the pyramid off the top of their heads, the general public still thinks of it as the basic foundation of a healthy diet. It seems pretty harmless, right?

It turns out the food pyramid was introduced by the U.S. Department of Agriculture and was heavily influenced by meat and dairy lobbyists. If you take a look at who works for the USDA and the FDA, you'll find that a lot of them used to be executives or lobbyists for the massive corporate conglomerates that make most of the food that is sold at your local supermarket. You have people who used to work at huge corporations like Monsanto, for example, only now their job is supposedly to protect us from corporations like…Monsanto.

To me, that sounds like a pretty good recipe for collusion. You have all these people weaving a web together and steering the message in a certain direction. You need milk for calcium. You need steak for iron. And so on. But the people who are preaching that message are mostly the same people who stand to profit when you buy the stuff they tell you to buy.

Reading stuff posted online by like-minded people not only continued to open my eyes about animal-based products, but also to processed corporate food. The dominoes started falling faster than ever.

I became more mindful of preservatives and artificial colors. Through social media, for example, I learned about Red #40, a food dye used in some of the biggest brands of yogurt, juice, energy drinks, candy and breakfast cereals.

Here are some fun facts about Red #40: It is derived from petroleum, which, as we all know, is a delicious and healthy source of food. It has been shown to alter the DNA of lab mice. Also, researchers have observed a strong relationship between the use of Red #40 in food products and the rise of ADD/ADHD in kids.

(I've noticed that Adderall, the drug they use to treat AD/HD, comes in a pink pill. I wonder if they use Red #40 to color them. Wouldn't it be ironic if they used Red #40 to color the Adderall they give to people who have ADD from consuming too much Red #40?)

In America, a strawberry sundae at McDonald's is artificially colored with Red #40. In England, where Red #40 is formally not recommended for children, that same McDonald's strawberry sundae is colored with strawberries. I know—crazy idea, right?

Although the Food and Drug Administration has approved Red #40 for human consumption, I decided that I don't need any food coloring bad enough to take that risk.

And Red #40 wasn't the only widely used product that got red-flagged from my diet. One by one, the more I learned, the more items I added to my own personal list of banned products.

I also learned about GMOs. So far, I don't think there's a ton of awareness about GMOs among the general public. In terms of name recognition, I'd say GMOs are probably where the word "organic" was ten years ago. But that's definitely starting to change.

GMOs (genetically modified organisms) are foods which have been genetically manipulated by scientists from their natural state. Genetic material gets doctored in a lab to make it easier for farmers to grow stuff—for example, by making the crops more resistant to pests.

There's a documentary I like a lot called *GMO OMG*. When it came out, I went and spoke at the red carpet premiere in Ocala, Florida.

At first, the filmmaker, Jeremy Seifert, wasn't intentionally trying to go on a crusade against genetically modified foods. He didn't have an agenda. He's not even a vegetarian. He's just a dad. Once his three kids came along, though, Jeremy and his wife realized they weren't just choosing food for themselves anymore. Jeremy's experiences raising—and feeding—his kids led him to do a little homework on mainstream foods. The more information he found, the fishier it all seemed. That research is what inspired the movie.

GMOs have been in use since the 1970s. Over 80% of the produce we now eat is genetically modified. Did you know that? I know I didn't, until I saw the film.

There are a wide range of opinions out there about how safe GMOs are. Truthfully, at this point, no one knows for sure if eating vegetables which have been genetically modified is harmful to humans.

But, as *GMO OMG* shows, the FDA only reviewed one study on the safety of GMOs before approving them for widespread use. That study was conducted over a period of six months— not nearly enough time to learn what a lifetime of eating GMOs might do to our bodies or to the environment.

Even worse, the study was conducted by Monsanto, the agricultural giant who stood to benefit the most from the approval of GMOs. The government basically outsourced the job of regulating Monsanto to Monsanto. So what kind of results do you think they came back with?

GMOs can take a lot of different forms. For example, unlike traditional non-organic corn, which gets sprayed with pesticides out in the field, one type of corn which Monsanto produced in a lab contains a pesticide literally inside the seed. The corn seed is actually labeled as a pesticide itself, because of what's inside it.

If I told you that particular variety of corn was used in the box of corn flakes in your cupboard right now, would you really feel good about feeding that cereal to your kids? Because this isn't science fiction. That's what's going on with the food you eat every single day. About three-fourths of all processed foods sold in groceries stores contain genetically modified ingredients.

And there is nothing on that box of corn flakes to let you know that the product inside is genetically modified. There's a huge battle underway to get GMO products labeled. And the food industry is doing everything it can to derail that legislation.

The companies who sell GMO products insist there's nothing dangerous or harmful about them. And yet those same companies have fought tooth and nail to resist labelling their packages and letting consumers know what they're eating. It seems only fair to wonder: If GMOs are safe, then why spend so many millions of dollars trying to shut down labeling? Why not be transparent? Shouldn't people have a choice?

In my experience, when people go out of their way to be secretive, it usually means they have something to hide. If you can't give me full disclosure on what you're trying to feed me, then I want no part of what you're selling. End of story.

To be fair, maybe the people who claim that GMOs are perfectly harmless will be proven right someday. But on the other hand, maybe there's a reason GMOs have been outlawed in multiple countries in Europe. (That's true, by the way. You can look it up.) If the evidence is inconclusive, I'm going to play it safe. I don't need to eat stuff that's banned in other countries in order to live my life to the fullest. Not by a longshot.

Practically speaking, in today's society, it is impossible to completely abstain from genetically modified foods. They're everywhere. But whenever I have a choice, I choose to eat non-GMO foods. It's the same way I approach organic foods. I just do the best I can under the circumstances.

Although I didn't originally give up meat for ethical reasons, the more I read, the more my vegetarianism started taking on an ethical dimension. When I drove past that factory farm in Texas with Crazy T, I was struck by how huge the place was, and how bad it stunk, and how many chickens I knew had to be inside. But I don't think I gave too much thought to what was actually going on in there at the time.

Once I started interacting with other people on the internet who really gave a shit about food, I was exposed to more information about just how inhumanely most of the animals people eat are treated. I started doing some research, and that led me to documentaries, and by watching those, I came face-to-face with the cruel reality of factory farming. I realized that even though I'm not some huge animal lover, I didn't want to contribute to a system that is okay with treating living creatures that way.

I also learned the full extent of how dangerous eating meat can be for your health, in ways I had never imagined. That gave me yet another reason to embrace the vegetarian lifestyle.

Originally, I had given up meat based on a gut conviction. But as I did more research, I felt my convictions strengthening. I realized there is basically no good reason to eat meat—and a lot of really great reasons not to. And increasingly, I also saw how that applied not only to meat, but to animal-based foods across the board.

All told, over a decade passed between when I became a vegetarian and when my diet went completely vegan. It was a really gradual process.

Although I didn't realize it when I first swore off those chicken breasts, there are lots of different kinds of vegetarians. Obviously, the biggest difference is between regular vegetarians, who don't eat meat, and vegans, who also don't eat any products that are derived from animals.

But that's just the tip of the iceberg. There are also pescetarians, who swear off land animals but still eat seafood. There are even some strict vegans who won't eat honey, since it comes from bees. When I first gave up meat, without realizing it, I became what's known as an ovo-lacto vegetarian.

Ovo-lactos don't eat meat, but they do eat eggs (ovo) and dairy (lacto). It all comes down to what you as an individual will and won't eat.

By 2010, I was still technically a vegetarian—not a vegan— but I had gradually given up foods that a quote-unquote "vegetarian" can still eat. In retrospect, pretty much from the time I gave up meat, I was already teetering on the brink of eating a fully plant-based diet.

For example, not long after I gave up meat, I also gave up

products which contain gelatin. Gelatin is in tons of really all-American foods, like Pop Tarts, but a lot of people probably don't realize what it is. When most people think of gelatin in its raw form, they probably just picture a packet of white powder. Maybe they even think it's a chemical or something. I definitely did not used to know.

Here's the ugly reality: Gelatin is an animal-based product, usually made out of cows or pigs. Manufacturers make it from a bunch of melted down scraps of cartilage, bone, skin, tendons, connective tissues, and so on—stuff that a lot of even the proudest meat eaters would want nothing to do with.

Early on, I also started abstaining from any foods that had chicken stock or beef stock in them. A lot of people might not realize it, but a lot of vegetarian foods—like vegetable ramen, for example—usually still contain animal stock. I just figured that if I didn't want to eat a chicken, then I didn't want to down the bathwater from a chicken carcass either.

Pretty quickly, I also swore off anything that contained lard, like refried beans. Lard is made out of pig fat, and after a while I couldn't see any difference between eating that and eating bacon.

Just as the idea of eating chickens had become unappetizing to me, back when I first started wrestling, slowly but surely that kind of thinking expanded to include other animal-based products. I had never been a huge milk fan, but the more I thought about it, the less I wanted anything to do with it. I realized I didn't really have any desire to consume this white stuff that got yanked out of a cow's udder. Eggs were always kind of weird to me. But now, more than ever, I no longer felt like scrambling up some chicken embryos and calling that breakfast.

I think a lot of people feel the same way, even if they don't want to admit it. It really comes down to what you're used to. Some people are weird about sushi, for example, because they weren't raised eating raw fish. Well, I bet if we weren't all raised drinking milk and eating cheese and eggs, most people wouldn't be willing to consume any of that stuff, even on a dare. But old habits die hard.

When it came to eating eggs, as late as 2010 I was still telling myself the same things I had told myself about those chicken breasts: You need the protein. Don't think about what it is. Just eat it.

When I went to a restaurant and they gave me eggs on a plate, already prepared, it wasn't that bad. But when I was the one cracking the shell, it was hard not to think about what it was or to ask myself whether or not I really needed to eat it.

For a long time, whenever I ate an egg, I would get a mental image of Fred Flintstone in the old cartoons, eating one of those humongous pterodactyl eggs. That's what eating an egg made me feel like. So I would do a little bit of role-playing. I would pretend I was a caveman and trick myself into believing I was okay with what I was doing.

For a while there, I was on and off with eggs. I would cut them out for a while, and then I'd try to wrap my head around them again and give them another go.

Cheese was kind of the same way. I mean, I'm from Wisconsin, the land of cheese, beer, and brats. And cheese, with all its fat and salt, tasted great. Sure, I didn't like milk, and if you think about it for a second, milk sounds even less appealing after someone cultures it and lets it mold and then turns it into cheese. But somehow I would disassociate milk and cheese from one another and cheese would get a pass.

Slowly but surely, though, my evolution continued. First, I gave up on cottage cheese. Then yogurt was next. But I would still sprinkle cheese on my food and use whey protein powders in my shakes.

That continued until I saw a documentary called *Forks Over Knives,* based on a book called *The China Study.* The book's author, T. Colin Campbell, is an American bio-chemist who was the lead scientist on the 20-year China-Oxford-Cornell Study, which linked the consumption of animal products, including dairy, to chronic diseases like coronary heart disease, diabetes, and various forms of cancer.

For me, that was the straw that broke the cow's back.

I threw out my parmesan cheese and replaced it with something called nutritional yeast. With a name like that, I know nutritional yeast doesn't sound too appealing. But it's actually got this really good, really nutty flavor. Plus, unlike parmesan, it's really good for you. So I started sprinkling that on my pasta instead. I also gave away all of my whey protein powders and replaced them with different plant-based protein powders. They tasted just as good and weren't any more expensive.

And with that, it was done. My long evolution—from full-time animal consumer to vegetarian to vegan—was complete.

Honestly, switching to a 100% plant-based diet wasn't a huge emotional moment in my life. I had been on the journey for some time. I was already teetering on the brink. *The China Study* was just the last little nudge that finally pushed me over the edge.

Meanwhile, in the ring, I was in the midst of becoming the longest reigning X Division Champion in the history of TNA. And I never actually lost that championship. Hulk Hogan gave me an ultimatum to hand over that title in exchange for a shot at the world title.

And then, on July 8th, 2012, I won the TNA World Heavyweight Championship over Bobby Roode at the Destination X pay-per-view event in Orlando.

Winning another organization's world title was certainly another career achievement. But becoming fully plant-based was just as significant to me. While one was a huge step in my professional career, swearing off animal products was a huge step in my personal evolution. It was an affirmation of my entire belief system and of what I hold to be true. It was a milestone on the road to becoming what I believe is a better me.

Ever since I was little, I had wanted to reject the conventional path that was laid out for my life. And as I had become more educated about food and started forming my own opinions, I came to see our mainstream food culture as just another dimension of society's rigid rules.

That culture was so firmly entrenched that, for a long time, I didn't even realize it was there. The whole time I was a kid, it didn't even dawn on me that there might be another path. Slowly but surely, I had come to see that the conventional wisdom about food was often wrong, and that there are way more—and way better—dietary options than you would ever be aware of just by scanning the shelves at your local neighborhood supermarket.

I came to realize that there might be a reason why, in high school, they only spend one semester teaching kids about food in health class. And why, even in that one semester, they don't really tell you the truth about the food we all eat.

Maybe it's because if they told you the real story, when you went down to the cafeteria afterwards, you might see that something was amiss. You might not stick your dollar in the soda machine or the candy machine—all the things the school administrators let inside their walls to try and take your money.

Back when I first started wrestling and getting in shape, existing on a solely plant-based diet would have seemed like an insane thing to do. But after all my hard work at the gym and in the ring, and after all of the hard work I had put into learning about food and then putting that knowledge into practice, I was in the best shape of my life.

In February of 2016, I signed with the WWE, the biggest sports entertainment entity on the planet. I was surprised to discover how many of the superstars on the WWE roster follow some variation on a plant-based diet. I was also pleasantly surprised to learn that the WWE is very mindful and respectful toward their athletes' dietary preferences, and provides catering that accommodates everyone. The organization has an ongoing commitment to feeding their wrestlers the kinds of foods that allow us to give our customers our best possible performance, every time out.

By the time I made it to the big time I was 37 years old. If I hadn't been taking care of myself and educating myself about the kind of nutrition my body truly wants to consume, would I have still had the physical goods to deliver in the ring at the highest level? I can't say for sure.

But I do know this: By swearing off eating animal products, I didn't lose any energy or stamina or strength, or go backwards according to any standard of measurement you might care to use.

Quite the contrary. I got better.

CHAPTER 4

So that's it. That's the story of where I come from, how I got where I am as a wrestler, and how I evolved from eating a typical Midwest American diet to being 100% plant-powered and free of chemical additives. That's my journey, up to this point anyway.

Now that you know the who, what, and where, I'd like to get into some of the how and the why. I'd like to share some of the information I've accumulated over the years and delve a little deeper into how I approach food.

If you're just reading this book because you're a wrestling fan, I guess this is the point where you might think about tuning out. But I hope you'll stick around and hear me out. I think you'll be glad you did.

Again, let me be clear about something: The purpose of this book isn't to try and make everybody go vegan. We all know that if that was my goal, I would maybe get 15 people to sign up for that plan.

I do hope some of you might be willing to think about switching to a plant-based diet, or at least about moving a little bit in that direction. Hell, if I could convince everyone reading this to plan just one meal a week that doesn't include animal products, I would consider this book a humongous success.

But to me, diet isn't just a question of whether or not to eat meat. Even if you have zero interest in a plant-based diet, I hope I can at least provide some food for thought about the things you choose to eat, whatever they may be.

When it comes to food, I don't think most people realize how much choice they really have. You'd never know it just by watching commercials on TV or by scanning the shelves at your local supermarket.

Just because you were raised eating a certain way, or because the FDA approves certain products, or because you see your favorite athlete on TV endorsing some fast food restaurant, that doesn't make a certain type of diet "right." As a matter of fact, if you devote a little time and energy to getting past the bullshit and the lies, you might be surprised to discover just how wrong the all-American diet really is.

I also don't think most people realize just how dangerous a lot of the most easily-accessible food options really are. As I see it, the vast majority of foods that people are being sold in this country are not really fit for human consumption.

I would go so far as to say that most people eat something at almost every meal that a lot of people—myself included—would consider poison. No, it won't make you keel over on the spot. But in the long run, I believe it takes its toll.

Whether you're interested in becoming more plant-based or not, everyone's diet would benefit from cutting out the scientifically-enhanced laboratory projects that the major food producers are shoving down our throats. If only, say, 20% of our food supply was bad for people, maybe I could look the other way. It's not like I eat perfectly nutritious food all the time.

But if I walk into a typical grocery store, there are maybe two aisles there that are of any use to me. Everything else I won't even touch. Your typical fast food or "fast casual" chain restaurant has even less to offer me. And that's not just because of the lack of vegan options. It's because of the quality of the food.

Maybe it's just me. Maybe I'm just a non-conformist. But personally, that makes me angry.

People need to wake up and start paying attention. They

need to stop trusting stores, restaurants, and corporations that do not have consumers' best interests at heart and who have no conscience about what they sell to you and to your children.

To be a little more direct: Take your head out of the sand. Eat like you give a damn. Eat like it matters what goes in your mouth, where it came from, what it does to your body, and what impact your food has on the larger ecosystem of planet Earth.

The information is out there, if you can be bothered to find it and then act on it.

Even if, for some reason, I woke up tomorrow and decided to eat meat, that wouldn't affect the way I purchase food or the way I make decisions about what I put in my body. Because to me, it's about more than just veganism. It's about being healthy. It's about being an informed consumer. And it's about not being taken advantage of.

The food that we eat should be the single most important thing in our lives. What you will and won't put in your body are not decisions to be taken lightly. The food we eat forms the core of everything we are. Literally.

Becoming a vegetarian and training for wrestling were the things that first drove me to learn about food and the food industry. You might well have different reasons for starting your own journey with food. Maybe you want to lose some weight or just feel a little healthier, or both. Maybe you want to seek out foods that are better for the environment or kinder to animals.

But if you feel like you might be in the dark when it comes to buying food, and you don't like how that feels, in this chapter I hope I can pass along some useful information. Maybe I can plant a few seeds in your mind and nudge you on a path toward some more enlightened dietary decisions.

During those first few months when I was training to become a wrestler, after workouts, a group of us guys used to head over to eat at our local Subway.

I remember there was one guy in the group who was really overweight. I guess he had decided being fat was his gimmick, so he committed himself to becoming even more humongous.

Actually, he wasn't just going for the fat gimmick. He was going for every gimmick known to man, all at the same time. The last time I saw him, he was wearing a hockey jersey and bringing a hockey stick with him into the ring. But he also had face paint on, and once in a while he would also have a chain around his neck. Sometimes he brought a chair, too. There was a lot of stuff going on there.

Anyway, that guy would waddle up to the counter and order a sandwich with double meat, double cheese, and double mayo, with no vegetables. He was basically eating a mayonnaise sandwich. Needless to say, it was disgusting.

Meanwhile, I would get the chicken breast on the whole wheat bun, thinking that was a solid, nutritious choice for me. (This was back before I gave up meat, obviously.) Fat boy might have been eating cholesterol bomb sandwiches. But back then, I believed I was doing the right thing. All of us guys were operating under the assumption that Subway is a good thing to eat. That's what they tell you in the commercials anyway. Eat fresh, right?

Well, I hate to break it to everybody, but Subway's really not that great for you. Sure, compared to other fast food joints, it might be the lesser of the two evils. But in no way, shape, or form do their commercials accurately represent what they're offering the public.

You see high-level athletes in their TV ads, and it's implied that those guys eat Subway as part of their training. (Of course, you should take that with a grain of salt. A lot of those same guys also endorse Coke and Sprite, and I doubt too many of them are cracking open a soda right before game time.)

But as you peel back the layers and read the ingredients, you start to uncover a very different story. When you really break it down, the overall nutritional value Subway offers isn't much better than the other fast food options.

You can eat relatively "healthy" at any fast food place—as long as you're just basing your decision on fat, protein, and carbohydrates. But in reality, there are so many other things to consider when it comes to health or nourishment.

Go find the ingredient list for the meat in that Subway chicken breast sandwich. Trust me—it doesn't just say "100% chicken" like it should. There are a bunch of fillers in there with the meat, including a couple of things you've probably never heard of or can even pronounce.

And by the way, the meat in that sandwich didn't just come from one animal. It came from thousands and thousands of chickens, all mixed up and pressed together into one "breast." And you probably don't want to know what kind of sad life all those chickens led before they ended up on your sandwich.

Then check out the bread—which, by the way, looks, tastes, and smells almost nothing like the bread they sell in bakeries, in case no one's noticed.

Until recently, bread at Subway contained azodicarbonamide, a chemical that's also commonly used in yoga mats, among other non-edible products. A woman named Vani Hari, AKA "The Food Babe," made a big stink about azodicarbonamide on the internet. She put on the full court press and started getting the word out. (She's a pretty good-looking chick, which probably helped the story get a little traction.) So Subway gave in and took that stuff out.

But even now, that doesn't mean you're eating wholesome whole wheat bread by any stretch of the imagination. There's still a bunch of ingredients in there that sound like they belong in a high school chemistry textbook.

Nowadays, I believe you can get a spinach leaf on your Subway sandwich instead of iceberg lettuce. I guess that's something. But it goes without saying that all the vegetables in your meal are GMO and non-organic.

Even after I gave up Taco Bell a few years back, I still continued to eat at Subway sometimes. I felt like that was the one place I could still get fast food, because they offered a veggie patty. I would get that veggie patty with some Southwest sauce, or some mustard or oil and vinegar.

By that point in my food education, I knew that eating Subway wasn't all that good for me. But it wasn't until I examined the ingredients that I understood the exact level of crap I was eating.

As a rule of thumb, the less ingredients a product has, the more natural it probably is. Well, a Subway veggie patty has almost 40 ingredients. Among the highlights: "Calcium caseinate." "Hydrolyzed corn." And the always intriguing and mysterious "natural flavors from non-meat sources."

If you really break it down, Subway is more like a science experiment than food. Compared to a Double Whopper with Cheese? Yeah, it's healthier. But compared to actual real nourishing food? Forget about it.

In a way, I think what Subway does is worse than what the other fast food places are doing. At least the other guys don't claim to be good for you. But Subway is the perfect example of the system trying to make you think you're eating right when everything they're feeding you is completely wrong.

Don't think they don't know what they're doing. This is not an accident. They're doing this on purpose. They're advertising one thing and then selling you something completely different. And I'm not trying to single out Subway. They're not alone. Between chain restaurants and store-bought food products, there are hundreds if not thousands of other brands like them.

All these companies are having the last laugh at our expense. The powers that be don't want you to realize you have better options. It took me a solid decade to see through all the lies and misinformation, and to figure out what kinds of foods I really should be eating.

If you're like most people, every day, at almost every meal, you are trusting corporations to make decisions about your health and well-being. Whether you consciously realize it or not, you are assuming that, as long as the FDA signs off on what corporations are selling us, the products can't be all that bad.

A couple generations ago, that might have been an okay strategy. But things have changed.

I don't think corporations are more evil today than they used to be. They've just gotten better at what they do. There are so many more additives and chemicals and preservatives and genetic food modifications at their disposal. And the average person's education and awareness about all that stuff is basically non-existent.

If I asked you if you'd be okay with drinking a soda that contains ingredients which are also used as a flame retardant, I'm pretty sure you'd say no. But no one's going to actually ask you that question. The FDA will just approve that stuff, and no one will hear about it until some food activist does some homework and then causes a stink about it on Facebook.

This isn't some hypothetical situation I'm describing here. Until recently, about 10% of all sodas sold in the U.S. contained brominated vegetable oil, a synthetic chemical which was first patented by companies who used it for fireproofing. Because it's believed to cause skin lesions, memory loss, and nerve disorders, brominated vegetable oil is banned throughout Europe, India, and Japan.

As it turns out, until very recently, when you were "doing the Dew," that's what you were really doing.

Now that there's some consumer outrage over trans fats and artificial colors and flame retardant sodas and breads that double as yoga mats, several big-name restaurants and food companies have made a big deal out of changing their recipes. And that's an encouraging sign. It shows there are some people out there who care about what they eat and drink. It also shows there are some corporations who feel like they have to make a few adjustments so they can keep their sales up.

But don't get it twisted. These corporations aren't changing their recipes because they've suddenly realized the error of their ways, like Ebenezer Scrooge on Christmas morning. It's because they do research on their customers, and they're afraid that they might lose market share if they don't make it look like they're changing with the times.

Despite whatever small changes might have happened recently, it's naïve to think that the food products big corporations sell are all good now. Consumers need to keep the pressure on and be aware of what actually goes into their food. Every time you spend a dollar on food, you voice your opinion in the only way that corporations pay attention to. When you spend your money on processed, unnatural crap, you tell them you're okay with it. So why would they have any reason to pursue real change?

They're only going to change as much as they have to in order to maintain their bottom line. And when it comes to selling wholesome, responsible, nutritious food, in my opinion, they've got a long, long way to go.

At the same time that corporations have been getting more and more sophisticated about using science to make food products, they've also been getting smarter about advertising. Places like McDonald's, to pick one example, spend ludicrous amounts of money perfecting even the tiniest details, like the color schemes of their restaurant decors and the designs for their logos, all because they're trying to send subliminal messages that make you want to keep coming back.

I don't think most people know that. And if most adults don't realize what McDonald's is up to, then what chance does a defenseless little kid have?

And make no mistake—McDonald's markets directly to kids. They know that if a rug rat begs and screams long and hard enough, eventually the parents will give in and take them to get a Happy Meal. And since kids can't drive themselves, when the parent goes through the drive-through to get their kid some McNuggets and a toy, the adult will probably get something for themselves, too.

We all know kids are very impressionable. Here's an inter-esting anecdote: Back in the 1930s, spinach sales shot up by 33% almost overnight. The driving force behind that sales spike was demand from kids.

And it wasn't because kids' taste buds changed. You know what it was? Popeye the Sailor Man, which began as a comic strip in 1929.

It's true. There's a town in Texas that has a statue of Popeye to this day because of what he did for spinach, which was the big local cash crop.

Popeye's creator, E.C. Segar, made Popeye love spinach because spinach is high in iron, and to Segar, that sounded like something that would make you strong. Then all these kids saw Popeye's muscles pop out from downing a can of spinach and thought, man, if I eat that stuff, I'm going to get big forearms and kick some ass.

To me, that story proves that, with the right marketing, you can sell kids absolutely anything—good or bad.

When I was a kid, I'm not even sure I really thought that McDonald's had the best-tasting food. The Golden Arches just had this aura around them. Eating at McDonald's was cool. It was a huge treat. That's what I was told in the commercials. And that's what I believed.

McDonald's will do anything they can to give kids happy childhood memories. They want to establish positive associa-tions with their food and their restaurants in young customers, so that when kids grow up, they'll bring their own kids. That's their whole modus operandi. Not only is the food kid-friendly, it also comes with a toy. And, of course, lots of McDonald's also have a pretty sweet playground attached.

When I was a kid, we used to pick up those hot cakes and sausages on the way to my grandma and grandpa's house. We'd all eat breakfast together and then go swim in the pool. Those are some great memories. And McDonald's is right smack dab in the middle of them.

Stuff like that is ingrained in a lot of our minds. And it didn't happen by accident. McDonald's was aggressively trying to make that happen.

And it's still going on. My mom has become a lot more aware of nutrition and eating since I was growing up. And yet still, if she spends the day with my nephews, there's a good chance Grandma DeeDee is taking everybody to Mickey D's.

I understand it. She wants to treat them. But by doing that, she's playing right into McDonald's' hands. She's continuing that tradition, even though the food McDonald's sells is in no way, shape, or form suitable for kids.

There's a good chance my nephews will grow up associating quality time with grandma with Quarter Pounders made out of pink slime. And then the cycle will continue.

(What's pink slime? Glad you asked. Within the meat industry, it's known as "lean, finely textured beef." In more straightforward terms, pink slime is a bunch of really gross fatty bits of leftover meat that are treated with ammonia gas to kill bacteria and then added to ground beef. McDonald's is far from the only food supplier guilty of using it. An estimated 70% of supermarket ground beef contains pink slime.)

I can't totally blame McDonald's and Subway and all the other big food corporations. There's nothing illegal about what they're doing (even if some of it should be). I understand that this is a democracy and a capitalist society. It's not McDonald's job to tell people not to take their kids to McDonald's.

Really, that should be the parents' job. But when today's parents were kids, their parents took them to McDonald's, too. No one ever told them just how bad McDonald's really is. So, realistically, how are most parents going to realize there's anything wrong with keeping that tradition alive?

What really bothers me is that neither our government nor anyone else with a platform in our society is trying to level the playing field for the average consumer. No one with a real voice is out there telling people that from the moment they're born corporate

America is looking at you purely as a consumer. From the minute a kid can understand a TV commercial, or recognize a picture of Elmo on a box of crackers, he or she is officially under siege.

No one is reminding people that when you see fun commercials on TV or appealing packaging in a grocery store, it's not because that company is your friend. It's because that company has spent a lot of time, money, and effort trying to craft a message that will deliberately mislead you and make you want to buy their crap. No one is trying to set people straight and tell them that the images surrounding the products they buy usually have very little relationship to the products themselves.

When our great-grandparents were back in the old country, food was something that came from the earth. It was natural. It was sustenance.

Now it's something that comes from a lab. And to the people who sell it, it's all just business.

I don't believe that the people who run massive food companies actually want to make people sick or fat. I'd like to believe they're not quite that evil. I'm pretty sure the person who runs Subway simply doesn't care about the quality of the food.

And in fairness, for all I know, the CEO of Subway doesn't know the first thing about diet and nutrition. I wouldn't assume the CEO of Subway or McDonald's is secretly living on a super clean macrobiotic diet when they get home from the office. They probably eat Oreos and drink Coke, just like everybody else.

It's not their job to be your mom or to be your conscience. The people who run food corporations are just thinking about food costs and profit margins. They're asking themselves, what is the cheapest possible way I can put something I can legally call chicken inside our chicken sandwich? Which is another way of saying: What is the lowest quality of mystery meat that our customers will stand for?

And then, once the company's food scientists finish developing a suitable space-age chicken-based foodstuff that test markets well enough, the CEO goes out and hires someone to make a TV commercial about how their company uses only the finest farm-raised chickens.

More often than not, it's just straight-up lies.

As a consumer, there are so many ways you can go wrong, even if you're sincerely trying to make an effort and eat right. I'm still learning myself, to this day. People really don't know the facts. When it comes to buying and eating food, they believe what they've been told. And in so many ways, the deck is stacked against you. There's so much information out there which has been designed specifically to mislead you.

That doesn't just apply to chain restaurants. It's everywhere, really. Maybe you're at a local mom and pop restaurant, and instead of a burger and fries you order the grilled chicken salad from the "Healthy Choices" section of the menu. That might seem like a solid decision. But if that salad is made with iceberg lettuce, then you're essentially just eating water and not getting the nutrients you need. If there's barbecue sauce on the chicken, then you're taking in a bunch of sugar. If you're using ranch dressing, well, then you might as well not bother at all. But the restaurant selling you that salad is more than happy to let you think you're doing the right thing.

Or maybe you buy a wheat bagel with fat-free cream cheese, thinking that's better than the regular stuff on regular bagels. It sure sounds good. But, for reasons I'm about to explain, most of the time it's really not any better. Not at all.

If you're going to navigate your way through all the misinformation being thrown your way as a consumer, you have to learn to see past all the dirty tricks. And to do that, you need to get a real education about nutrition—the one you should have gotten in school.

It's not always easy—or even possible—to find out what's going on inside restaurant food. That's why the best place to start is your local supermarket.

You're going to need to learn how to shop for groceries—the right way.

Many people consider companies like Kraft and General Mills (to name a couple of the biggies at random) respectable brand names. A lot of these brands have been around for generations. We all grew up with them in our kitchens and on our dinner tables. We feel comfortable eating their food.

But personally, I don't trust the big food manufacturers, and I don't trust most of the products they sell, whether they're vegan or not.

If I find myself browsing in a typical neighborhood grocery store, my first rule of thumb is to ignore everything it says on the front of food packages. Generally speaking, if it says something on the front of a package, that's not real information—it's advertising. It's propaganda. Companies will tell you whatever you want to hear so they can get you to put their stuff in your cart.

Whether an item is billed as "sugar-free," "fat-free," "light," or "all-natural," those terms don't necessarily mean what you think they mean, and they don't always mean the product is good for you. They don't mean anything, really. They're just buzzwords. They're there to make people think that they're making a healthier choice. They're there to make you feel good. But they're mostly lies.

Some of the absolute worst offenders are the food products which pass themselves off as healthy. Sure, everybody knows that donuts are bad for you. But when people buy a loaf of whole wheat bread, they like to think they're buying something that's better than Wonder Bread.

Store brands of wheat bread always have these really wholesome-sounding names, like "Earth's Bounty" or "Nature's Reward." But in reality, there isn't much difference between those loaves and the really bad stuff. It's Subway versus Burger King all over again. Usually, the manufacturer just altered the ingredients enough to let them write some advertising propaganda on the front of the packaging. They're selling you their not-so-bad stuff on the premise that it will kill you a tiny bit slower than their really bad stuff.

(Trust me. All those Healthy Choice entrées in the frozen section of the supermarket are far from the healthiest choice you could be making.)

For example, if a product says "all-natural," you might assume that means it's healthy, right? Well, no, not exactly. Wood is natural. So is wool. That doesn't mean those are things you should be putting in your body.

And those aren't just random made-up examples. You might be eating more of both of those things than you realize. They use cellulose (made out of wood) and also cotton as a cheap, non-fattening filler in shredded cheese, salad dressing, ice cream, and more.

And just so I don't come across biased here, let me mention that they also put wood pulp in a lot of organic products, too, because it has a lot of fiber, which makes products seem extra healthy.

That's why I say you have to read the labels and know what they mean. Wood and cotton may well be "natural" and "organic." But that doesn't mean I need them in my salad.

Take the example of "Natural Red 4," a food coloring you will often find in ingredient lists at your local supermarket. Natural Red 4 is derived from the bodily secretions of a parasitic insect called a cochineal. If you've ever had ruby red grapefruit juice, you are acquainted with Natural Red 4, whether you're aware of it or not. To release the coloring, the insects are powdered and then, usually, boiled in ammonia. But, since insects are "natural," Natural Red 4 is legally labeled an "all-natural" food product.

You know that shiny shell on the outside of a lot of candies? It's often made from shellac, a resin secreted by an Asian insect known as the lac bug. They also use it to coat pills and coffee beans and even to put that waxy sheen on apples and other fruits and vegetables.

Want more examples? Lanolin, an oil which sheep produce in their wool, is identified on packages as "gum base." It's used to soften foods.

A tasty-sounding product called L-cysteine is used as a dough softener in lots of mass-manufactured bakery goods like bread, cookie dough, and pies. And according to a 2007 investigation, although there are lots of ways to make L-cysteine, about 90% of the L-cysteine Americans eat is made out of duck feathers.

Mmm. Parasites. Secretions. Feathers. They're all-natural. And boy, do they sound delicious. Am I right?

"All-natural" is only one of many terms that don't always mean what you might think they do. I've seen candy corn labeled "fat-free." And technically, that's true. Candy corn doesn't contain any fat. But it's also mainly made out of sugar. And guess what? After you eat the candy corn, that sugar is going to turn into fat and then you're going to get fatter.

Or sometimes, you'll see a product like low-fat cheese. Cheese, by its nature, is a very fatty food. So if your cheese is low-fat, then you've got to wonder what the hell they put in there instead of the fat. Was it a bunch of fillers? And if so, what are they? And are you even sure that stuff will be better for you in the long run than just plain old fat?

And there's more. "Sugar-free" doesn't mean a product isn't sweetened. It usually just means the manufacturer used artificial sweeteners instead. And, as I've mentioned, it turns out sugar substitutes might be just as bad for you as regular sugar. There's some evidence that our bodies process fake sugar the same way as real sugar. It's been shown that people who switch to sugar substitutes on average don't weigh any less than they did before the switch. Perhaps most troubling of all, as most people know, sugar substitutes are made in a lab and, in some cases, have been linked to cancer.

All of my research and experience has convinced me that our bodies want to digest minimally-processed foods that are natural and come from the earth. Artificial sweeteners represent the exact opposite of that. And yet they have the FDA's full seal of approval.

The bottom line here is that you need to stop giving your groceries the benefit of the doubt. If a stranger walked up to you on the street, handed you some food, and said, "Eat this," there's no way you would do it. You wouldn't ask yourself if it smelled good, or if it tasted good, or if it was inside a cool box. You would want to know what the food was made of.

And that's the same way you need to approach store-bought food. You don't know who the hell is selling you that product or what's inside that box, and you need to proceed with caution.

To get at the real information, you need to flip the package over. In my experience, unless you can find definite proof on the back of the box that something is good for you, then you should assume it's not. Everything else on the packaging is just there to trick you.

There are a number of questions you should be asking yourself when you read the back of a product. Does it say organic? Is it non-GMO? What about the other nutritional content? Is it really high in sodium or sugar, for example?

A big lesson I've learned is that when you eat packaged foods, the shorter the ingredients list, the better. How many preservatives and fillers are in the ingredients list? Can you recognize or even just pronounce all the items on the list? As a rule of thumb, if you see a word you don't know on the back of a label, chances are it's something that you and your body don't need.

Once again, this applies just as much to store-bought vegetarian options as it does to products which contain animals. Just because something is vegetarian or vegan doesn't make it healthy.

When I first swore off those chicken breasts, way back when, I switched to a lot of vegetarian meat substitutes. In the beginning, a lot of those came from a company called MorningStar Farms.

MorningStar is the biggest producer of vegetarian foods in the U.S. But it's also owned by Kellogg's, and that means it has some of the same issues as many other mass-produced foods. MorningStar foods contain genetically modified ingredients, such as soy. They also have suspiciously long ingredients lists and are very high in sodium.

Ten years ago, companies like MorningStar, Boca, and Garden Burger were the only quick-fix options vegetarians had. But now there are better options. So I tend to avoid the old standbys.

Most people have probably glanced at the nutritional info on the back of a package at least once or twice. But very few people really know what they're looking at, or what they're looking for. I sure as heck didn't when I first started reading labels.

To show you what I'm talking about, let's pick some basic staple products from your local grocery store, flip them over, take a look at the back of the packaging, and see what's really going on inside.

We'll start with some mass-produced grocery store whole wheat bread.

Whole wheat. Sounds really healthy, right? Well, let's compare it to the stuff I buy and then we'll see:

One slice of a well-known national brand of whole wheat bread contains:

- 100 calories
- 1 gram of fat
- 7% of your daily recommended sodium intake
- 7% of your daily recommended carbs
- 3 grams of fiber
- 3 grams of sugar
- 3 grams of protein

For comparison's sake, the bread I buy has only one gram of

sugar per slice. That's 2 extra grams of sugar per slice, multiplied by however many slices there are in the loaf. If there are 20 slices of bread, that's an extra and unnecessary 40 grams of sugar in every loaf of bread that you probably didn't realize you've been eating.

Also, I get 6 grams of protein per slice in my bread, which is twice as much as there is in this conventional mass-produced loaf.

All in all, though, that's not too bad so far. But now let's take a look at the ingredients.

The first ingredient listed in the typical store brand is whole wheat flour, which is what you want. But then the next ingredient is unbleached enriched wheat flour, which is the standard junk they use in most mass-produced breads.

Ideally, whole wheat bread should contain 100% whole wheat flour and not include the unbleached enriched wheat flour. But that would probably cost the manufacturer more money. And since the manufacturer did use some legitimate whole wheat flour, they get to call their product whole wheat bread, and people are none the wiser that their bread isn't exactly what they think it is.

Working our way down through the ingredients, next we come to sugar and then molasses—which is also sugar—then calcium propionate, which is a preservative, several fillers, and then some whey and some nonfat milk. If you bought this bread, you're consuming dairy, whether you realize it or not. All in all, your bread contains over 30 ingredients.

Now let's look at the ingredients in the bread I buy: It contains sprouted wheat, water, whole raisins, wheat gluten, lentils, yeast, and salt. That's it. Seven ingredients. All of them are organic, and I know exactly what all seven of those things are.

As you can see, whole wheat bread is not all created equal. When we looked at the nutritional information, the two breads weren't all that different, really. But when you compare the ingredients lists, the difference is massive.

Now let's take a peek under the hoods of two different brands of peanut butter. Just like with the bread, when you look at the nutritional information, all peanut butter is going to look pretty much the same. You'll have about 15 grams of fat per serving and about 7 grams of protein. Your carbs will vary depending on how much sugar is inside.

Once again, the devil is in the details, on the ingredients list. The major store brand contains roasted peanuts, sugar, molasses, fully hydrogenated vegetable oil, grape seed or soybean oil, and salt, in that order.

For comparison's sake, the peanut butter I buy contains one ingredient: Peanuts.

Basically, the manufacturers of the name brand peanut butter have added a bunch of unnecessary crap just so they can sweeten their product and make it cheaper to produce by using less peanuts.

We've always been told that "choosy moms choose Jif." Well, if that's the case, it would appear that choosy moms have no idea what the fuck they're talking about.

Fully hydrogenated vegetable oils are added to give store brands of peanut butter their creamy consistency. The stuff that I buy separates when it sits on the shelf. When you open the jar of my stuff, there's oil on top and you need to stir it up before you use it. It can be a pain in the ass to mix it up. I'm not going to lie. It's not as convenient as the other stuff.

But it's a pretty widely accepted scientific fact that fully hydrogenated vegetable oils, which contain saturated fat, are really, really bad for you. And personally, the convenience factor is not nearly enough to make me eat an ingredient that's bad for my body. I'll just take a second and stir up my peanut butter before I eat it, thank you.

The same goes for the sugar and molasses in the mass-produced peanut butter brand. To me, it's just not necessary.

If you put a mass-produced brand of peanut butter side by side with my stuff and then ask a kid to pick which one they want, obviously the kid's going to go with the sweet and creamy stuff every time. We're predisposed to seek out fats and sugars, because when we were still hunter-gatherers, foods that had the most sugar and fat and calories gave us the most bang for our buck.

We crave that stuff. It's in our biology. And corporations know that. So they're going to sneak a little extra sugar and fat and salt in there to try and sell you their product—or, more accurately, to sell it to your kid—even though it's no good for us.

If you try peanut butter that's just made from peanuts, you will notice a difference in taste at first, for sure. You might miss that sweetness. But if you stick with my brand, I promise you your taste buds will adjust. And don't forget, a lot of times you eat peanut butter with jelly or with bananas, both of which are already very sweet to begin with.

If you gave my peanut butter a shot for a while, you might well decide you hate it and go back to the old-school stuff with all the sugar, the molasses, the hydrogenated oils, and the salt. That's fine. It's your decision.

On the other hand, you might find that you acquire a taste for my stuff and that you enjoy the feeling you get from eating a healthier, more wholesome product. Hell, eventually, you might decide to buy a Vitamix, dump some peanuts in there, and then make your own peanut butter (or almond butter or cashew butter). Then you know exactly what you're eating.

My point here isn't to make you feel bad or stupid for eating Skippy. At the end of day, the amount of sugar in the name-brand peanut butter isn't enormous.

I just want to show you that national brands of peanut butter aren't as harmless as they might seem. My goal is to make you realize you have choices and to encourage you to do some research and to make informed decisions. By making a bunch of little changes, I find you can eliminate a large amount of unnecessary bullshit from your diet pretty painlessly.

Now let's take a look at a popular kids' cereal.

Like a lot of people, I grew up eating a ton of sugary cereals. I was in a hotel somewhere recently and I got my hands on one of those single-serving boxes of Fruity Pebbles. I used to love this stuff. And it was vegan. I'll admit, I was a little tempted.

Nobody is perfect 100% of the time. Personally, I operate on something called the 80/20 Rule. The 80/20 Rule means that 80% of the time I try to be smart about what I eat, when I eat, and how much I eat. The other 20% of the time, I eat whatever the hell I want. 80/20. I find that's a good rule of thumb.

It's something I came up with a while back. I enjoy food. I want to enjoy my life. I feel like if you put the work in and you're usually mindful about what you eat then you should also reward yourself. It's impossible to be on point all the time. And it's not a lot of fun.

The cool thing about the 80/20 Rule is that it allows me to eat that 20% without any guilt. When people binge on greasy fast food or sugary desserts, a lot of times it seems like they regret it before they're even done, because they know it's so bad for them.

But not me. I know I'm making good dietary decisions overall, so I can eat some fun food without worrying about it afterward.

Anyway, there I was in that hotel, all set to have at those Fruity Pebbles. But then I flipped over the box and looked at the ingredients. That changed my mind in a hurry. I wouldn't eat that crap if you paid me to. (Okay, fine. But you'd have to pay me a lot.)

Here's what's inside Fruity Pebbles (which, just as a reminder, are based on a lovable children's cartoon character): Rice, sugar, hydrogenated vegetable oil, coconut and palm kernel oils, salt, natural and artificial flavor, red 40, yellow 6, turmeric oleoresin (a food coloring), blue number 1, yellow number 5, blue number 2, and BHA.

Just like with the peanut butter, we're talking about a lot of sugar, fat, and salt. We know those things aren't good for us. But corporations know we have a hard time saying no to them, so there they are, front and center.

More importantly, BHA is a preservative which is suspected of causing cancer. And Red #40, as we've already discussed, has been linked to ADD/ADHD in kids.

There is no shortage of food experts—most of them tied to the food industry—who will dispute that Red #40 is dangerous and who will say that you need to consume a ton of BHA for it to be bad for you.

But let me flip that around and ask a few questions: How badly do I need to eat that stuff? Why on earth would I choose to take any sort of health risk just so I can eat an artificial food coloring? More importantly, why would you take that risk with your children?

Why would you give corporations and the government the benefit of the doubt? What have they done to earn that trust?

And why the hell would a manufacturer use potentially harmful ingredients when, in most cases, there are no-risk natural alternatives? It's probably because the manufacturer cares more about saving a couple pennies than about your kid's welfare.

To me, giving kids Fruity Pebbles is way more serious than adults choosing to eat at Subway. If you go to Subway, that's you making a minor dietary miscalculation for yourself. But if we're talking about something like a typical sugary kids' cereal, then that's a massive mistake. And it's not for you. It's for your children.

If you're a parent, you might end up having a really scary conversation with a doctor one day, all because you let your kid eat this stuff. But hey, it comes with a toy, right?

Even the guilty pleasures I allow myself within the 80/20 Rule are regulated by some overall rules of what I will and won't put in my body. If you want to have a piece of cake, I say have a piece of cake. If you want to have a cookie, have a cookie. But even if you're enjoying some empty calories, that doesn't mean you have to give in to The Man and eat some poisonous garbage.

And there are safer alternatives. Personally, I also like Cocoa Puffs. The problem is that Cocoa Puffs have all the same crap as

Fruity Pebbles. And as much I like Cocoa Puffs, I don't like them enough to put my health at risk.

Luckily, there's a company that makes an organic all-natural version of Cocoa Puffs. Just because it's organic doesn't mean it's health food. It's still got a bunch of sugar. Nutritionally, there's nothing really good going on in there. But it's way better than the General Mills version.

I am willing to allot myself a certain amount of sugar in my diet. But my personal daily allotment of potentially life-threatening preservatives and food coloring is zero. When it comes to that stuff, I'm out.

Is the organic version of Cocoa Puffs a little more expensive? Sure. But if you wait until it's on sale, you can stock up then, and you'll be able to satisfy your craving for Cocoa Puffs—without the risk of giving yourself cancer.

It has always amazed me that some of the absolute worst foods on the market are the ones that are targeted at kids. We have these breakfast cereals and snack cakes and whatever else, and they have zero redeeming nutritional value. But somehow it's supposed to be okay. Why? Because it's "kids' food." Kids like to eat that stuff. So I guess that makes it okay that your 3-year-old just pounded 60 grams of sugar in one sitting?

Kids want that stuff because they see it on TV. TV markets the products towards the kids because, even though the parents have the wallet, the kids have the influence. The kids whine about it, and then the parents buy it to shut them up, even though it's grossly unhealthy.

Don't worry, people think. He's just eating those Lucky Charms because he's a little kid. Eventually, he'll become an adult and eat Grape Nuts instead. That's the logic, I guess?

Well, I reject the concept of "kids' food" entirely. There are two only kinds of food: Good food and bad food.

If you're a parent, it's up to you to expose your kids to the right kind of diet. It's our responsibility as adults to teach kids that you can't just base what you eat on gluttony and flavor alone. I'm not a parent. But it seems pretty obvious to me that kids should be eating the absolute best, healthiest food you can get your hands on. Instead, they're eating the worst. I don't see how you can just give that crap a free pass.

The commercials and the sugar and the prizes inside all hook kids in. And then that kid grows up and has kids of his own and feels nostalgic when he sees a commercial with an animated leprechaun in it. So he buys his kids a box of edible garbage, and the cycle repeats itself. It's that McDonald's phenomenon all over again.

Breakfast for a growing little human becomes nothing more than GMO corn, sugar, and artificial colors. But somehow, it's okay because there are colored marshmallows and a cartoon character on the box.

As a culture, we have a huge blind spot about how much damage you can do to your kids with the foods you allow them to eat. Recently, the NFL player Adrian Peterson caused a bunch of outrage because he disciplined one of his kids with a switch. Some people view that as child abuse.

I didn't find that as offensive as some other people did. Back when I was a kid, I definitely got hit when I got out of line. My nose got bloodied more than once. And looking back, I'm glad it was. I feel like facing physical consequences from time to time for acting up had more of an effect on me than I would have gotten from getting a time out or having a videogame taken away from me.

But here's my point: When the news came out about Adrian Peterson, everyone was up in arms. He should be suspended. He should be banned for life.

Okay, I get that. But let's say Adrian Peterson didn't hit his kid with a switch. Let's say instead he fed the kid a bunch of sugary cereals and crappy foods, and then the doctor told him his kid had diabetes. Would *SportsCenter* have been covering that story every night?

Because as far as I'm concerned, letting an 8-year-old kid become obese and sick is definitely child abuse. And yet it happens every day, in every town, and you don't hear all that much outrage about it.

If you physically discipline a child, in a few days the bruise will go away. But if your kid develops diabetes, that's permanent. Even if the kid doesn't develop an illness, if they're obese, they're going to face an uphill battle in life. They'll get made fun of at school. They'll never get to enjoy physical activity the way they should have.

To me, that's way worse than a couple whacks with a switch.

Here's something else to think about: Some cities, like New York and Los Angeles, issue every restaurant a letter grade based on cleanliness. An "A" means they're all good. A "B" means the place might be a little sketchy. And a "C" means they might be storing their burger patties in the employee bathroom or something.

No one in their right mind would choose to bring their kids inside a restaurant that had a "C" hanging outside. That would make them feel like a bad parent.

But when it comes to nutrition, most fast food restaurants are a "C" at best. And yet you see whole families piling inside for some burgers or fried chicken on their way home from Little League. Most breakfast cereals as just as bad. And yet they're just as popular and just as All-American.

Maybe, at the end of the day, people just don't give a fuck. But I'd like to think it's just that people haven't been given a reason to give a fuck. They don't truly understand what they're up against, or how many other options they truly have.

By the time people reach adulthood, it's usually too late to change their perspective about nutrition. Once you're out on your own, your diet and your attitudes about food and your buying habits are usually pretty well established.

It needs to start when you're young. Instead of all the useless information we force on kids in school, we should give them real, practical information about nutrition. It blows my mind that I wasn't educated about this stuff back when I was in school. As far as I know, to this day, we're still not teaching kids the things they really need to know about food.

We all want our kids to be happy and healthy and to live life to the fullest. But the most important thing in life is our health, and, outside of genetic factors no one can control, the most essential building block of health is our diet.

We teach our kids to get good grades so that they can go to college and have careers and make money, so that they can then buy cars and houses and a bunch of toys. But later in life, if their health fails them, we know all those things will be meaningless.

From as soon as kids are old enough to understand, we should be teaching them that every meal they eat is an important decision. Just like we teach them to look both ways when they cross the street, we should teach them they have to understand exactly what they're eating—and why—every time they break bread.

When they grow up, they should have the tools to make well-informed decisions. If they still decide to eat McDonald's every day or drink soda with every meal, that's cool. It's a free country. That's their prerogative.

But let's let people choose the food they eat with a little transparency, so everybody knows exactly what they're doing. Is that too much to ask? Maybe that would save some college kids from starting their adult life behind the eight ball, packing on that Freshman Fifteen the second they leave home.

If it was up to me, I would also teach kids that eating meat isn't a given. There's no law written in stone that says humans were meant to eat meat or animal products. That's what this society has traditionally deemed acceptable. But that's not the case everywhere, or for everyone.

Think about it: If you put a little kid in a pen with a baby pig, a baby cow, a baby dog, and a baby cat, the kid isn't going to want to pet the dog and the cat, but eat the pig and the cow. Those are learned behaviors. Eating meat is a custom that each individual has a choice to either participate in or to reject.

I don't think teaching kids to take food seriously and to consider vegetarianism would solve all the world's problems. But at least it might plant some seeds in their minds. It might encourage a few more kids to keep their eyes open and dig a little further into what they eat and where it comes from. They might grow up judging food on more than just how it tastes, how cheap it is, and whether or not they can get it at a drive-through.

So far, I hope I've given you some motivation to get a deeper, more informed education about food. Although I personally choose to embrace a plant-based diet, I would never try to force that on anyone else. I just want you to open your mind, learn what options you really have, and see where that takes you.

I know that if I asked you to go vegan right now, you'd almost definitely say no. But if I just ask you to dig deep and learn the reality of the food we eat in American society, I hope you'll maybe say yes.

And guess what? I believe that's where I'll get you.

Once you learn all the things I've learned, I won't be surprised in the slightest if you call me a couple years later and tell me you've become a vegan. I know for a fact that the more you learn, the less you are going to want to eat meat and other animal-based products. You'll naturally become more plant-based. It will take care of itself.

If you really find out what's going on with the food most people eat, and you think hard about what's right for you and your long-term health, I think slowly but surely you'll find yourself evolving in the same direction that I have. It won't happen over-night. It took me over ten years.

But it will happen. And when it does, it won't be something that bums you out. It won't make you sad that you're not eating cheeseburgers anymore.

It will make you feel good to know that you're taking control of your diet, instead of letting someone else tell you what to do and then laughing all the way to the bank.

And it will make you happy knowing that the healthy, nourishing food you're putting inside your body is what your body has really been wanting all along.

CHAPTER 5

There's an old joke:

Q: How do you know if someone's a vegan?

A: Don't worry. They'll tell you.

Good one, right?

Ever since I stopped eating meat, I've tried to avoid becoming one of those cliché self-righteous vegetarian assholes who sometimes give the rest of us a bad name. I've always hoped people would respect the decisions I've made about food. And in return, I try to respect everybody else's.

Unless someone asks about my diet, I usually don't go into it. But seeing as how you've made it this far, I'm going to assume you're at least mildly curious about why I've chosen to pursue a plant-based existence.

So get ready. This is the part you've probably been waiting for, where I climb up on my soapbox and turn into a big ol' preachy vegan douche. I'm going to tell you all the reasons why I believe eating animal products is a really bad idea, and all the reasons why I believe so strongly in a plant-powered lifestyle.

Don't worry. I won't slip in any graphic pictures of sad little pigs and cows. But I might paint a pretty unhappy picture of an animal-based diet.

When you're a professional entertainer or an athlete—or in

my case, both—eating and training are a huge part of everyday life. People in my line of work spend a big chunk of our time shopping for food, prepping meals, eating meals, working out, and recovering from working out. We share those parts of our lives on social media, and in turn, those things become part of our public identity.

As I've become part of a community of people—both online and in real life—that includes lots of high-level athletes and body builders, I've encountered a number of buff dudes and girls who are vegan. Some of them have been eating that way their whole life. There are more of us out there than you probably realize.

But as we all know, when people talk about veganism, the typical image that comes to mind isn't someone with a decent physique and some muscle mass. It's definitely not a professional wrestler.

So when I publicly identified myself as an herbivore a few years back, that very quickly set me apart. When people thought of me, veganism became a big part of who I was in their minds.

And as you might imagine, when I first announced that I had switched to a 100% plant-based diet, I heard a wide spectrum of reactions.

Of course, there are always going to be that vocal few who have to say something to try and stir the pot. "Why don't you eat meat, you pussy?" Something clever like that. Some people just like typing the most ignorant, negative thing their little pea brains can come up with while they're sitting there on the toilet playing with their phone.

That kind of stuff rolls off my back pretty easily. If you're that guy, go ahead and eat all the chicken-fried steak you want. Of course, twenty-five years from now, when you have high blood pressure or diabetes or a heart attack, I don't think it's cool that I'm going to have to chip in for your healthcare because of all of your bad decisions. But blast away. I can take it.

Knuckleheads aside, the overall reaction has been pretty civil.

In fact, my experience has shown me just how many people want to know more about the subject. Put it this way: If everyone who's ever asked me about my diet buys a copy of this book, I'll sell enough copies to break even. And that's all I really care about.

Before we get into the reasons why I choose to not eat animal products, let me get a couple of things out of the way:

First of all, I'm not trying to be all holier-than-thou here. I'd like to think I have a pretty healthy lifestyle, but not everything I put in my body is the absolute optimal human fuel, especially for a pro athlete.

Being plant-based doesn't mean you have to be perfect. Believe it or not, there are people who follow way more extreme diets than I do. There are vegans who stick to whole food diets. That basically means they only eat foods with one ingredient, like fruits and vegetables and whole grains.

I'm still striving to learn more and to improve my diet, but at least for the time being I still eat food that's convenient, and sometimes that means processed foods like frozen burritos and store-bought meat substitutes. Just because those products are vegan doesn't magically mean they're great for me. Processed food is processed food. But those kinds of foods help me remain plant-based without completely changing everything in my diet and giving up all the types of food I like to eat.

I can still have a "chicken" sandwich. Or I can have a Tofurkey roast beef sandwich, and I can mimic the Horsey Sauce from Arby's with Vegenaise and horseradish. That way, I can replicate the flavor of that crap I used to eat in college—only minus all the crap.

Secondly, I don't want to come across as a hypocrite. I like to smoke marijuana. And I like to have a drink from time to time. And from time to time, I like to have a lot of drinks. There are people who might not drink or smoke weed who could point a finger at me for preaching about health and nutrition given the other stuff I do.

I just believe that everyone has to pick their poisons. We should all try to counterbalance the bad things we eat and drink with a lot more good things. In my estimation, it's way better for me to drink and smoke weed and eat clean than it would be for me to give up all intoxicants but then go and eat like shit.

Lastly, my objective here isn't to try to "prove" that everybody should eat the same way I do. I'm just telling you why I've made the decisions I've made.

I know some people might call bullshit on a lot of the things I believe. Trust me, I've heard all the arguments and all the counterarguments, too.

We all know any scientific study can be skewed to show whatever interpretation you want it to show. Anyone who's ever used Facebook knows that if you want to defend an opinion, you can always find some cherry-picked so-called "facts" on the internet to back you up.

I just want to share some information that I happen to believe about meat and dairy. I know full well that, if you wanted to, you could throw a different set of arguments back in my face to try and prove me wrong. If you don't want to believe me, there isn't much I can to do change your mind.

But for me, it's not about proving who's right and who's wrong. Here's the way I look at it: At the end of the day, none of us really has it all figured out. There are some fundamental truths we can all agree on. We know the earth is round. We know that the law of gravity is real. But otherwise, most "facts" are up for grabs. There's always going to be some new study or some new evidence overturning all the stuff we thought we knew.

So I choose to operate on the assumption that where there's smoke there's fire. If I read that a certain food might be bad for me, I ask myself how much I really need that food, given the potential risk.

I also base what I believe on the evidence I see with my own eyes. When I lived in Clearwater, Florida, I used to shop at a grocery store called Nature's Food Patch. The name pretty much says it all—it was basically just a smaller, independent version of Whole Foods Market. Next door to Nature's Food Patch, in the same strip mall, there was a Family Dollar store and a Save-a-Lot.

In terms of dietary priorities, you couldn't find two more opposite extremes than the people who shared that parking lot. Some of those people were there because they were committed to eating foods that met a certain standard of quality. And some of those people were trying to stretch a buck to feed their family, any way they could.

I'm not saying that to be judgmental. That's how it was for my mom and dad, back when I was growing up. Hell, that's how it was for me back when I was in college, packing on the Freshman Fifteen, and even when I first started training to be a wrestler.

But I remember that, looking at people getting out of their cars in that parking lot, it usually wasn't too hard to tell who was going to Nature's Food Patch and who was going to the other two places. And to me, seeing is believing.

If you're okay with letting the system and TV commercials and The Man tell you what you should and should not eat, that's your prerogative. But personally, I'd prefer to figure things out for myself.

Most people were probably raised eating the same kinds of foods I was. We were all programmed to look at food a certain way.

Hundreds of millions of dollars' worth of advertising gets thrown your way every year to try to maintain the status quo and make you believe that an animal-based diet is the only way to live your life. They are shoving meat down your throat, both literally and figuratively.

But I'm here to tell you that there's another way.

The system taught us to eat animals and animal products. But each of us has the power to accept or reject that habit. Our culture teaches us that we kill and eat some animals, like cows, pigs, and chickens, but we let dogs and cats sleep in our beds with us. But that doesn't make that type of thinking correct.

Our diet didn't get handed down to Moses, carved on a stone tablet. Somebody made it up. And more and more these days, it's the corporations that tell us what we do and don't eat, based on nothing more than their own bottom line. When it comes to food, there's no such thing as "the way it is." Someone decided how things should be, and then we were all trained to believe it.

No one comes out of the womb craving cows or pigs or chickens or cow's milk. That's something human beings invented. Although it might be easy to forget sometimes, eating animals is a learned behavior. And it can be unlearned, too. I'm living, breathing, pro-wrestling proof.

When people have questions about why I've chosen to eat the way I do—and I've heard plenty of them—here's what I tell them:

First, let's talk about some of the negatives that have been associated with eating meat and dairy.

I've already mentioned *The China Study*. Research conducted over the course of two decades by T. Colin Campbell and his son Thomas M. Campbell II showed a strong relationship between meat and dairy consumption and instances of certain illnesses. Compared to the Western world, people from areas of China that consume relatively small amounts of meat and dairy have significantly lower rates of diabetes, coronary heart disease, and several different kinds of cancer.

T. Colin Campbell didn't go into his research with any pre-conceived notions. He wasn't trying to prove a hypothesis he had already come up with. He just wanted an explanation for why cancer rates differed so much between different countries. And that's the answer came up with.

To me, it's kind of common sense that eating a lot of meat and dairy would probably have negative long-term health consequences. Compared to vegetables, meat—and especially red meat—is very hard for the body to digest. Compared to plant-based food, meat is also high in saturated fat, cholesterol, and other gnarly stuff.

But *The China Study* demonstrated in cold hard numbers that the more meat and dairy people eat, the sicker they get. As more and more people in China have adopted more Western-style diets, more of them have gotten sick from Western-style diseases. It's about that simple.

The documentary *Forks over Knives* followed up on T. Colin Campbell's work on *The China Study,* but also talks about a guy named Dr. Caldwell Esselstyn. Dr. Esselstyn grew up on a cattle farm in upstate New York, and, like most of us, he grew up believing that beef and dairy were part of a normal healthy diet. But later on, after conducting extensive research, he came to the conclusion that a lot of the things he had learned growing up had been dead wrong.

Based on his data, Dr. Esselstyn determined that, contrary to popular belief, milk most definitely does not do a body good. As a matter of fact, as bad as eating meat is for your body, consuming dairy products might be even worse.

Really give this some thought: We are the only species of animal that consumes other animals' milk. Cow's milk was not intended for human consumption. Literally. Our body is just not designed to process milk that was really intended for calves.

By the time we're adults, we simply don't have the enzyme to properly break it down. Go ahead and look it up. Some people are straight-up lactose intolerant. But even those of us who are able to digest lactose still suffer from bloating, indigestion, and other even more unsavory side effects as a result of consuming dairy.

The phrase "lactose intolerant" kind of cracks me up, to be honest with you. Is it really surprising your body doesn't want to process cow's milk? Why should it? You're not a cow. It's like saying you're bleach-intolerant or poison-intolerant. If you're lactose-in-tolerant, maybe there's nothing wrong with you. Maybe you just weren't supposed to be drinking that crap in the first place.

Despite what you might guess, neither Dr. Esselstyn nor T. Colin Campbell fit the stereotypes of new-age hippie crackpots. They're both respected professionals in their field. Bill Clinton, of all people, turned vegan after reading *The China Study*.

(Of course, I'm pretty sure Bill's still puffing those cigars. Like I said, you have to pick your poisons.)

And more importantly, neither Esselstyn nor Campbell knew what the other guy was up to until they found out about each other and discovered that they had come to the same conclusions. That made both of them realize that they must be on to something.

I also have my own theory about dairy. I don't know if there's any science to back me up, but the way I look at it, if milk promotes growth, and if you continue to consume it after you're done growing, then wouldn't it promote other kinds of growth— like cancerous cells and tumors? If you're leading an unhealthy lifestyle, or just taking in all the pollution and toxins that come from living here on planet Earth in the 21st century, then maybe consuming dairy might contribute to the growth of unhealthy things in your body. Who knows? Maybe that's one of the reasons the cancer rate is so high these days.

I subscribe to the theory that every time you put food in your mouth, you're either fighting disease or feeding disease. And I feel pretty confident telling you that milk isn't helping your body fight jack shit.

Forks Over Knives also documents how people suffering from chronic diseases radically improved their lives by changing their diet. One of people profiled is a guy who had heart problems and diabetes. The guy eliminated animal products from his diet and got in shape. As a result, he was able to stop taking four or five different medications and lead a healthy normal life.

The movie also shows a woman who went from competing in triathlons to suffering from a supposedly untreatable form of cancer. The woman switched from conventional doctors to a physician who prescribed a treatment centered around a whole food plant-based diet, and the new diet completely turned her illness around. By the time the documentary was filmed, she had been cancer-free for 15 years and was still out there doing triathlons at 55 years old.

Obviously, no one's saying that everyone who eats meat is going to get a disease and die young.

There are people who abuse their bodies in every possible way and somehow still live to be 100. But I have personally come across many, many examples of lives which have been saved thanks to plant-based diets.

I have a friend named Margarita Restrepo. Before I met her, Margarita was engaged to a healthy, active man named Thomas who was diagnosed with brain cancer.

In an effort to fight his illness, Thomas switched to a plant-based diet. Margarita made the switch, too, just to be supportive. Shortly after both of them changed their diets, doctors discovered that Thomas's tumor had shrunk significantly. The doctors were shocked by how much he had improved. They couldn't believe that simply eliminating animal-based foods had helped him get that much better that quickly.

Although Thomas ultimately lost his battle with cancer, Margarita's experiences by his side made a lasting impression. It gave her a completely different perspective on her diet.

She went on to start a magazine called *Naked Food*. The magazine isn't about veganism, although Margarita still adheres to a plant-based diet. It isn't about the ethics of what we eat either, although I'm sure Margarita loves animals just as much as anyone else. Her magazine is about peeling back the nutritional realities of what we eat, what we *should* be eating, and why.

In my experience, people are very skeptical when you try to tell them why meat and dairy and processed foods might be worse for their health than they realize. But very often, those same people are completely willing to accept any shred of evidence that suggests certain types of 'alternative' plant-based foods might be a bad idea.

Have you heard the one about how drinking soy milk and eating tofu makes dudes produce a bunch of estrogen and grow man boobs? I know I have. About a thousand times.

People were really quick to jump on that bandwagon. But here are the facts: Soy has never been linked with excess estrogen production in men. There is a possible link between soy and excess estrogen in women, but—and this is the important part—it's not the organic whole tofu I eat once or twice a day that might be causing problems. It's the processed GMO soy isolates and soy byproducts manufacturers are sticking in your food as fillers.

Which means this: If you don't eat tofu and don't drink soy milk, but you do eat a bunch of mass-produced store-bought products and foods served by big chain restaurants, you're currently eating way more of the potentially bad soy products than I am.

Hell, I can make it even more straightforward than that: If soy really made dudes grow tits (or if marijuana does the same thing, because I've heard that one as well), then by now, I'd have a big old pair of double D's.

Don't believe the hype. Don't accept something on faith just because you heard your buddy say it one time. Do a little digging. Thanks to the internet, it's never been easier to find some legitimate information.

Unlike the bogus tofu-man-boobs theory, there are all sorts of credible data strongly suggesting that the paths to lots and lots of diseases are accelerated by eating meat and dairy. I think most people will acknowledge that eating too much meat is unhealthy. But I don't think most people realize just how unhealthy an animal-based diet can be.

One study, conducted over the course of two decades, compared vegetarians to meat eaters. And the results were pretty straightforward: At the end of the 20 years, the vegetarians had outlived the meat eaters. And what's more, the more meat people had eaten over those 20 years, the more likely they were to have died.

The negative effects of a meat-eating lifestyle show up in all kinds of ways. For example, one in three meat eaters will die from a heart-related illness. On the other hand, heart disease among vegans is extremely rare bordering on non-existent. One study found that people with cholesterol levels below 150 don't get heart disease. And the average vegan's cholesterol level comes in around 130.

In my experience, the same goes for blood pressure. Every time I get my blood pressure checked with a bunch of other wrestlers, mine is usually the lowest. And that's a pretty healthy group of people we're taking about.

If someone smokes their whole life and then dies of lung cancer, everyone assumes that smoking killed them, right? And yet if a guy eats barbecue all the time and then get gets colon cancer, people might still be a little bit skeptical about a link. Maybe you would be, too. Well, let's look into that.

Kerry McCarthy, a member of British Parliament (and a vegan), made a stir recently after she advocated for the use of tobacco-style warnings on non-vegetarian food.

Sound crazy? Actually, the risks associated with smoking and with eating meat may be more similar than you realize. According to a 2014 study conducted at University of Southern California, eating a diet heavy in animal proteins during middle age makes you four times more likely to die of cancer. That isn't much different than the differences in lung cancer rates between smokers and non-smokers.

The BBC recently invited a doctor named Michael Mosley (who is a meat eater) to sift through a whole bunch of literature and scientific data to try to uncover the health implications of eating meat. You know how they say that every time you smoke a cigarette you take fifteen minutes off your life? Well, Dr. Mosley concluded that every time you eat a sandwich that includes bacon, you lose one hour.

And if that's not a credible enough source for you, then how about the World Health Organization? They recently linked red meat to cancer, and classified processed and cured meats as carcinogens, right alongside cigarettes.

Maybe meat and tobacco aren't all that different after all. Maybe it really is time we started looking at meat more like the way we look at cigarettes. Nobody's telling people they can't smoke. But the people who are selling you that stuff should be transparent about the risks you're taking so you can make an informed, grown-up decision.

Tobacco executives knew the truth about cigarettes for years, but they denied it as long as they could. I suspect the meat and dairy industries know more than they're letting on, too, but just like Big Tobacco, they're going to keep their mouths shut even if that means a bunch of people will die younger than they should have.

The government has the power to change things if it wants to. In my lifetime, people used to be able to smoke everywhere, from restaurants to airplanes. You could even light up in hospitals. But first, the government made all the smokers go outside, and now they're making people stand farther and farther from the entrances of buildings.

You also see all those ads on TV nowadays telling kids that smoking isn't cool. I don't know the stats, but based on the eye test, smoking seems to be waning. It seems like it's not as acceptable among young people. It's certainly not as popular as it was when I was a kid.

I'd like to believe the same thing might be possible when it comes to eating meat and other animal products. And yet our government still actively promotes an animal-based diet. The U.S. Department of Agriculture played a hands-on role in massive ad campaigns like, "Beef: It's what's for dinner" and "Milk: It does a body good."

As if it's not bad enough that the government promotes an animal-based diet, they also don't do a very good job of regulating the quality of the animal products people eat. Supermarket beef is pretty commonly contaminated with fecal matter. And unless you're buying organic grass-fed beef, you're also eating meat that contains antibiotics, pesticides, and hormones.

Farm-raised fish (which means most of the fish sold in stores and restaurants) contains antibiotics, too, and even ocean-caught fish frequently contains high levels of mercury.

According to the *New York Times,* when researchers from Johns Hopkins tested a bunch of chickens for antibiotic levels a few years back, they found traces of antibiotics which are supposed to be illegal because they can help breed antibiotic-resistant "superbugs" that can kill humans.

But that's not all. The researchers also found a whole lot of other unwholesome stuff in the chickens that they weren't even looking for. For example, they found caffeine and the active ingredients in both Benadryl and Prozac.

Why would chickens need antidepressants? So they don't freak out too bad about spending their short, miserable lives inside a tiny cage. (Although it's not like the factory farmers care about the chickens' mental health. Apparently, they just discovered that stress makes chicken meat get kind of tough.)

The idea is to keep the chickens awake, alert, and focused on eating as much as possible. Time is money. The producer wants the chickens to grow up and get fat as quickly as possible so they can be killed and sold. And then the process repeats itself, over and over and over. The animal becomes nothing more than a commodity.

Did I mention those same researchers found arsenic in the chickens, too?

Yup, you read that right. Arsenic was added to chicken feed for years, because it was said to make chicken flesh looker pinker and more appetizing. Once word spread around the internet, Pfizer, the manufacturer of the arsenic-laced chicken feed additive (and also the good ol' country folks behind such drugs as Viagra, Lipitor, and Zoloft) agreed to stop selling it. Until then, there was arsenic in as much as 70% of the chickens sold in America.

I would never say you can't eat meat and be healthy. Tons of people have built great physiques eating clean diets which include chicken and fish and even red meat. I can't argue with the results.

But for me, a plant-based diet isn't just about avoiding cancer and other potentially food-related diseases. Now that we've gone over some of the negative consequences associated with the meat-centric diet most of us grew up with, let's talk about some of the positives that come with making informed changes.

In the beginning, my journey might have been about health. But as I learn more, it's also about trying to be an ethical member of humankind. Living my life the way I do makes me feel better about myself and about the role I play on this planet.

Unlike a lot of people in the vegan and vegetarian communities, I am not the world's biggest animal lover. I don't spend my free time saving stray puppies and kittens. I always joke that I'm the only vegan on earth who doesn't own any pets. As I like to tell people: I don't choose to live with any animals—I just don't like eating them.

I hate even using the word vegan to describe myself, because I do use some animal products. I still have a leather steering wheel in my car. I still wear leather wrestling boots. What can I tell you? It grosses me out a lot more to eat animals than to wear them on my feet.

Until you start doing some research, you would never know how many consumer goods contain animals. There's an endless number of products containing cow parts alone. The system raises and kills hundreds of millions of animals for food. I guess it's just bad business to let all those scraps go to waste.

The list of uses for cows goes on and on. And it gets pretty grisly. Cow brains are used in anti-aging creams. They make adhesives out of cow blood. They put hooves in drywall. Cow hair is in air filters. And that's just the tip of the (really gross) iceberg. Some deodorants use cow fat. So do some lubricants. So if you're allergic to latex and you use a sheepskin condom and some cow-based lube, congratulations my friend, you're almost committing bestiality.

Even when it comes to diet, I'm not a true vegan in every sense. For example, I drink wine and beer, even though some of those aren't considered vegan.

A lot of beers and wines are filtered using a product called isinglass, which is made out of fish bladders. It makes alcoholic drinks look less cloudy. Legally, alcohol companies don't have to list ingredients on their products. So unless you do a little digging, there's no way you'd ever know that they used fish bladders to brew your pint of lager.

I prefer to drink vegan alcoholic beverages if I can. But I'm not anal about it. The fish bladders get filtered out before the booze reaches the bottle, so I'm not actually consuming any animal products. My objection is more on moral grounds. If I had a choice, I'd rather drink a cloudy beer than have a fish die on my behalf. But unfortunately, that's not always an option.

Eliminating every product that contains animals from your life is next to impossible. Just keeping track of them all is a challenge. I tip my hat to people who try to lead truly 100% vegan lives, but personally, I just do the best I can.

That's why I just prefer to say that I follow a plant-based diet. I don't eat animal products to the best of my ability. I'm not naïve enough to think that when I go out and eat at restaurants, absolutely everything's been quarantined off from everything else. That's just not the reality of the world we live in, at least not yet. But I do the best I can.

And I like knowing that, as much as possible, I don't participate in a system that unnecessarily slaughters so many millions of animals. I have an option to not contribute to their needless torture and death, so I choose to exercise that option.

It feels good to sit down and eat a meal knowing nothing had to suffer for me to eat and sustain my life. I think there's something really cool about that.

I believe animals aren't much different than us. I believe they can think and feel. I think they experience fear and happiness and pain and love, the same as we do. We just don't speak the same language as them. That's all.

I may not be a huge animal freak, and maybe I don't own a dog that I dress up in clothes to post on Instagram. But I still can't watch videos of animals being mistreated and not feel an emotional response. I'd like to think that even the most alpha male, macho, hunting and fishing kind of guy would cringe at the site of animals being tortured, or being raised as food in conditions which even the untrained eye can see are inadequate. I don't think that makes me especially compassionate. I just think it makes me human.

Maybe some people don't know those kinds of videos exist—even though they're not hard to find on the internet. But whether or not you've seen any footage firsthand, at this point most people probably have a pretty good idea how the vast majority of our livestock is treated. And yet hundreds of millions of people choose to play dumb.

The crazy thing is that many of those same people would consider themselves animal lovers. It's amazing to me when you meet one of these animal rights activists who go on and on about how much they love their doggies and kitties. But when you try to explain how much animal cruelty goes on in the meat industry, they tune you out. These people love to post pictures of that adorable kitten they rescued last week. But then, when it's time for lunch, they want their waiter to put some meat on their plate, and they don't want to know the first thing about how it got there.

It's been estimated that eating a vegan diet saves 200 animal lives every year. So congratulations if you found a home for a couple of cute little puppies this week on Facebook. Personally, I saved a bunch of animals myself this week, just by not eating them. And I didn't just spare the cute ones. And then I also didn't waste a bunch of time patting myself on the back on the internet.

From the perspective of someone who doesn't eat animals, some of the double standards I see are amazing. Go to any big function thrown by the Humane Society, look at the food they're serving, and I bet you'll see cold cuts and chicken fingers. People will literally have conversations about saving poor defenseless animals, all while chewing on poor defenseless animals. They should rename themselves the Cute Puppies and Kittens Society. Because as far as I can tell, those are the only animals the Humane Society chooses to be humane toward.

The ultimate example of the hypocrisy our society shows toward animals has to be the Michael Vick saga.

Look, I get it: Making dogs fight for money is sick. We all understand it's a thing that happens among certain groups of people and in certain cultures. But there is a broad agreement among both vegans and non-vegans in this country that dog fighting is not cool.

When that story broke, Michael Vick became public enemy #1. He went to jail, and people protested when he got back in the NFL. I'm sure he still hears boos to this day. And with good reason.

But as I see it, most of us are guilty of stuff that's almost as bad as anything Michael Vick did. Vick—and the guys he was involved with—tortured dogs because watching them fight brought them some pleasure. Those guys could have just watched a movie or gone to a strip club or something. But instead, they did something that involved animal abuse.

Okay, fine. But what about the leather seats in all of our cars? They don't need to be leather. They could just as easily be made from something other than animal skin. Wouldn't you say the cows they use to make car seats are tortured and killed for our pleasure?

And what about steaks and burgers? I'm living proof that human beings don't need to eat cows to stay alive and be healthy. So isn't the entire beef industry just about torturing animals for human enjoyment?

When the Olympics were held in Sochi, I remember seeing Keith Olbermann hopping up on his high horse on ESPN because the Russians had killed a bunch of stray dogs while they were building all of the Olympic facilities. I totally agree it's fucked up that a bunch of dogs died unnecessarily. But how many animals died that day in American slaughterhouses just so all the people who were watching Olbermann on TV could eat dinner?

Or what about every 4th of July, when ESPN—the same channel that broadcasts Keith Olbermann—shows Kobayashi pounding 50 hot dogs in ten minutes? Did the animals in those hot dogs die for any reason other than our amusement?

There are almost a billion people alive right now on this planet who could desperately use that food. And Kobayashi and Joey Chestnut's bodies probably aren't even going to get a chance to process whatever traces of useful nutrients might be inside those Nathan's hot dogs. Odds are those guys are going to go barf those franks up the first chance they get. That's not senseless violence against animals?

Most people are responsible for killing just as many animals as Michael Vick was. The difference between Michael Vick and the average carnivore is just that Michael Vick didn't get someone else to pull the trigger for him.

People like to think of themselves as the top of the food chain. Oh, yeah? Then go kill a lion with your bare hands. The fact is, nowadays we eat what someone else raised and killed and skinned and cleaned (and more often than not even cooked) for us. In today's world, the vast majority of meat-eaters are scavengers.

That's the difference between us and primitive man. We outsource our animal torture so that we don't have to see it or get any blood on our hands. When we had to kill animals for ourselves, we probably had a little more respect for our food.

But people don't want to raise their own chicken, and then kill it and eat it. They don't even want to get their own eggs. They want all of the dirty work to happen out of sight so they can keep it out of mind.

I already mentioned the animal carcasses I saw hanging in those butcher shops down in Mexico. But you don't need to travel that far to get a taste of what I'm talking about. If you've ever been to the Chinatown area of a big city, you've probably seen roasted ducks hanging in the windows of restaurants. Obviously, the restaurant owners aren't putting them there to gross people out or keep customers away. They're there to make people want to come inside and eat the ducks.

But in mainstream American society, a lot of people don't want to see the duck. They don't want any reminder that the food they're eating used to be a living, breathing, thinking, feeling animal. And the people selling chicken nuggets are more than happy to accommodate you, as long as you keep coming back for more.

That mindset is probably the reason people have made up so many words for the animals we eat. Think about it: We don't eat "pig," we eat "pork" or "ham." We don't eat "cows," we eat "beef." A lot of times we call chicken by its name. But then again, sometimes we also call it "poultry." As a society, it's like we've gone out of our way to put blinders on.

What if they called it a "cowburger?" Does that still sound mouth-watering?

The powers that be don't really want you thinking about what you're doing. And from what I've seen, that's fine by most people. They don't want to think about it either. Just put that "hamburger" on a bun with some lettuce and tomato and catsup, and let's call it a day.

We've all been raised to think very selfishly and to believe that we're the center of the universe. And our food system is the perfect example of that. Most of us rarely take time to really think about what it takes to manufacture, process, and deliver us all the food we eat (and all the food we throw away, too).

Have you ever considered the life of a dairy cow, for example? If not, here's how it works in a nutshell: Just like humans, a cow needs to get pregnant to give milk. So once she reaches adulthood, a cow is held in place with a specialized restraint (a dairy industry innovation that is sometimes called a "rape rack") and artificially inseminated.

Once the cow gives birth, her baby gets taken away from her. She then gets mechanically raped again and again, and has her babies taken away again and again, so that they're able to keep pulling milk out of her for the duration of her life.

Mechanical rape. Let that phrase rattle around in your head for a minute.

It's sad. Actually, it's more than sad. It's incredibly fucked up. It's sadistic. And if you consume dairy, then I hate to break it to you, but you're a part of that cycle of abuse.

Just think, if you gave up consuming cow milk, how many cow rapes could you stop?

To be fair, more and more people nowadays do make an effort. Many people are happy to tell you that they buy cage-free eggs or free-range meat. But for the most part, when you look behind the curtain, you find out that those words often don't mean very much. Like so many other terms we see proudly stamped on food packaging, they're mainly just marketing ploys.

Here are some facts: In the U.S., free-range just means that the animals have been allowed access to the outside. USDA regulations don't specify the size of the outside area or how much time the animal has access to it. According to the law of our land, the company that raises and sells the chickens gets to decide all that. So basically, just like Monsanto and their pesticide-filled corn seeds, our entire free-range poultry industry is operating on the honor system.

And that's just the free-range chickens. The less fortunate birds live and die in endless rows of tiny cages. In all likelihood, that's what was going on inside that factory farm I drove past in Texas with my friend Crazy T all those years ago.

In places like that, the chickens are fattened up so quickly that their legs can't support their body weight. They stay crammed in one position throughout their short, miserable lives, until, by the time they're killed, they're the equivalent of a 300-pound 3-year-old child.

And it's just as bad for cattle. Cows get crammed into these horrible living conditions, and then they're only fed corn, which is not their natural diet. The government subsidizes corn, so there's plenty of it, and it all has to go somewhere. So we cram it all down cows' throats.

Do you think cows don't realize what's going on? Do you think they're happy to be there? Do you really think they're that stupid? I sure as hell don't.

And then you have the people who raise these animals, and who also kill them. When animals live in such huge numbers in such large-scale facilities, they come to be seen as commodities. As products. And once the people who work there no longer see the animals as living creatures who are worthy of respect, you inevitably get cruelty and abuse. Sadly, that's just human nature.

As the world's population grows, and as more and more people around the globe can afford to eat meat, the demand for animal products continues to skyrocket. It's not my Grandpa Manny and Grandma Mary Jo raising these animals anymore. Those days are over.

Now it's huge corporations. And in a globally competitive market, with shareholders to report back to, well, corporations can't afford to have a conscience.

The sad part is that it doesn't have to be this way. As a matter of fact, if just a slightly larger percentage of people stopped relying on animals for food, our world would become unimaginably better.

That might sound like a crazy thing to say. But it's 100% true. And I can prove it.

It's hard to fathom just how much meat we go through in this country. In 2012, total meat production in America reached more than 93 billion pounds. I got these numbers straight from the horse's mouth, so to speak—The North American Meat Institute, which bills itself as "One Unified Voice for Meat and Poultry Companies Large and Small." They're not trying to freak people out about how much meat Americans eat. They're *bragging* about it.

Americans eat more meat than any other country on the earth—on average, 200 pounds per person per year. Most people I know would like to slim down. Well, if you're looking to drop five or ten pounds, here's some advice: Maybe don't eat 200 pounds of meat this year.

Forty-five million animals are killed every day for food. That's almost two million per hour, every hour, around the clock, 365 days a year.

I don't think most people truly understand the amount of resources that go into making all that meat. (And again, the powers that be don't want you to know, or to spend too much time thinking about it.) So much is wasted to feed so few people.

A full 70% of the grain produced in the U.S. goes to feeding animals. It takes an estimated 16 pounds of grain just to produce one pound of meat.

That's why it's not an exaggeration to say that if more people moved to plant-based diets, we could instantly solve world hunger. We wouldn't even need everyone to make the switch. If everyone went vegan overnight, and all the plant-based food we feed to cows, chickens, and pigs went directly to hungry people, we would actually have too much food.

If we cut out the middleman, and all the crops we use to

feed livestock worldwide were consumed directly by humans, there would be enough food to sustain an additional four billion hungry people—which is a couple billion more hungry people than actually currently exist in the world.

That's why I say that we don't need a planet full of devout vegans. According to experts, if as little as 10-20% of the world's population changed to plant-based diets, it's entirely possible to eliminate starvation worldwide.

And that's not the only way that producing meat is astoundingly wasteful. It takes a bunch of water and land to grow all that grain and other animal feed. And then we turn around and use more land and water while we feed it to livestock. In the case of cows and pigs, this goes on for years, until the animals are big enough for slaughter.

Every year, we keep hearing about droughts on the news, particularly where I live in Southern California. Everyone seems to act like there's nothing we can do about it. Well, did you know that more than half of the water we consume in the U.S. goes to raising and killing animals?

I've seen a lot of stuff online about how much water it takes to grow almonds. How come I've never seen anything about how much water it takes to raise livestock? It takes an estimated 268 gallons of water to make a pound of chicken. That's not a whole chicken. That's per *pound*. 576 gallons of water get poured into every pound of pork. And that's nothing compared to cows, which yield one pound of beef for every 1,800 gallons of water.

There are still some places on earth where eating meat is a necessity. Eskimos, for example, live on seals and walruses because they don't have access to plant-based options. That's totally fine by me. That's completely understandable. Trust me; if you and me are stranded together on a desert island with nothing to eat, I am going to eat the shit out of you, with zero second thoughts. That's a different set of circumstances. That's survival mode.

But in the world that we live in, eating meat is not necessary, regardless of what you may have been told.

And there's more: If more people swore off meat and dairy, that would also go a long way toward saving the environment. It's been said that you can't be a true environmentalist and still eat animal products. And I think there's probably a lot of truth to that. A lot of people might think they're environmentally friendly because they recycle and they drive a Prius. But it can be argued that the type of food you eat has a bigger impact on the planet than any other aspect of your life.

You know how some health food products are labelled "sustainable"? Those ought to tell you that everything else on the shelves and in restaurants is not sustainable—meaning, if we keep up the status quo, our whole food system is eventually bound to collapse.

Currently, more than half of the farmable land in the world is used to raise livestock. 26% alone is used for grazing, and another 33% goes to raising plants to feed animals. Meanwhile, a plant-based diet only requires one-third of the land needed to support a meat and dairy diet.

Central American rainforests were nearly destroyed to make grazing land for the cows that get eaten here in America and in Europe. On the other hand, it's estimated that every vegan saves an acre of forest every year, just by being plant-based.

It takes nine times more fossil fuels to produce one calorie of meat than it does to produce a calorie of plant protein. To put that in some kind of perspective, it takes the same amount of fossil fuels to produce a hamburger as it takes to drive a car twenty miles.

I know I'm lobbing a lot of numbers and facts at you. But if you don't believe me, go ahead and look them all up.

When we talk about global warming or climate change, people always think of cars and planes. But emissions from our food industry are incredibly destructive as well. There are almost 100 million cows in the U.S. at any given time, and cow emissions contain methane, which is really harmful to the environment.

I don't know if we're able to measure the total volume of cow farts going up into the atmosphere every year. But I can tell you that livestock produce 130 times more excrement than the entire human population. So we are talking about a shit-ton of cow shit here.

Yes, I know how it sounds when I say that cow farts are destroying the planet. Cows dropping ass. It sounds ridiculous. I get it.

And I'm sure the food industry would love for you to just make another joke about it and move on. But guess what? All those hilarious cow farts are messing up our planet, just so you can eat your rib eyes and your sirloins and your ice cream and yogurt and cheese.

In America, we like to think of ourselves as world leaders. Well, if we're really number one, and if we have it all figured out, then why don't we cut back on animal products and use our example to lead the fight against world hunger, disease, climate change, and animal cruelty?

We like to think we're so evolved and enlightened as a species. And yet one simple answer to so many of our biggest problems is staring us right in the face.

Beyond ending world hunger and saving the planet, if more people switched to a plant-based diet, imagine all of the health benefits we would see. For the reasons I've already explained, you would immediately see massive decreases in obesity and heart disease, and probably cancer, too.

But there's a lot more to living than just not dying. By switching to a plant-based diet, how much could you improve your quality of life?

I'm nowhere close to the age where people usually start getting heart disease and diabetes, so it's too soon to tell if I've spared myself from the ailments associated with a crappy diet (although I like my chances). But I believe that my plant-based lifestyle has already improved my health immensely, especially when it comes to recovering from injuries.

Whenever I get my blood levels checked, the inflammation markers in my body are basically non-detectable. Doctors have told me it's because of what I eat—or, more accurately, what I don't eat. Animal products are acidic, whereas plant products are alkaline. I'm always beating up my body and causing inflammation, but because of the way I eat, when I do get injured, there's no pre-existing inflammation compounding the injury.

And some would just say the proof's in the pudding. I'm 38 years old. But if you look at me, I don't think I look 38. If you watch me in the ring, I don't move like I'm 38. I'm still doing all the athletic stuff I used to do. I can still do 450s off the top rope. Sure, I'm a little smarter about it now, because I want to extend my career. But physically, I can still do all the stuff I used to do, and—knock on wood—I haven't really had any chronic injuries.

I believe that the longer I stick with a plant-based diet, the better my body will become. They say all the cells in your body die and get replaced every seven years. If that's the case, then there isn't one cell in my body that was made out of nutrients that my body got from digesting meat. And within a couple years, I won't have any cells that came from dairy, either.

Every day is a new opportunity to start doing the same thing for yourself. By becoming plant-based, you can replenish yourself down to the cellular level. You can clear out all the dog shit that never should have gone in your body in the first place.

You can literally become a whole new and improved person.

CHAPTER 6

Since I became vegetarian over a decade ago, I think I've had a positive effect on the way some of the people I know look at food.

My brother has become a vegetarian. My old buddy Justin is basically a vegan now. And my sister is a pescetarian, meaning she eats dairy, eggs, and fish, but no other animal meat. Sometimes she'll text me pictures of some vegan breakfast she made for herself and her kids.

My mom has never fully taken to my newfangled cuisine. It's harder for people of my parents' generation, because they weren't raised thinking about stuff like organic food and GMOs. But she's made real efforts here and there to get herself on a better track. She buys some meatless stuff now and then. And when she goes grocery shopping, she likes to send me pictures of all the organic produce she buys. I think that's really cool.

My dad doesn't eat healthy by any stretch. But he's added more vegetables to his diet, and he'll eat a salad now and then. Plus, he doesn't pile salt on his food anymore. Not coincidentally, he used to have high blood pressure, but he doesn't anymore.

I'd like to think all these people have benefitted from my example. Over the years, they've seen firsthand that, even with a plant-based diet, I still get to eat normal, good-tasting food. They've heard me ranting about GMOs or chemical food additives or what have you. But then later on, when they've spent some time poking around online, they've seen for themselves that I'm not just making these things up.

In the beginning, they might not have been inclined to follow my lead. But I think I may have planted some seeds and gotten the gears in their minds turning a bit, even if it was several years before any of them actually took the plunge and made some concrete changes.

And that's the whole reason I wrote this book: Just to tell you my story, and, in the process, to try and get you thinking.

Like I said way back on page one, ever since word got around that I eat a plant-based diet, whenever I do an interview, veganism has been one of the major topics that come up.

By now, hopefully I've shown you that the decision to give up eating animal products isn't as weird or as difficult as some people make it out to be. I hope I've also demonstrated just how dangerous an animal-based diet can be, and on the other hand, how beneficial a plant-based lifestyle really is.

Now that you know a little more about how I arrived at the decisions I've made about food, if you're thinking a wholesome, healthy plant-based diet could someday be right for you, let's take a deeper look at some of those cliché interview questions I've heard so many times:

So, if you're a vegan, does that mean you just live on lettuce, carrots, and brown rice?

Contrary to popular belief, vegans do not live on a steady diet of leafy greens. Personally, I barely eat lettuce at all. There's no nutritional value to iceberg lettuce, really. It's just crunchy water. (As a rule of thumb, the darker the leaf, the more nutritious your greens are.)

Consuming a plant-based diet does not mean living on rabbit food. I don't have to limit myself to raw veggies and brown rice at every meal, like some people seem to think. There are tons of different delicious and nutritious plant-based foods out there which can easily provide all the sustenance and caloric intake you need.

Let me flip it around, actually. Some people assume that eating a plant-based dieting is limiting. But I am willing to bet that I have more variety in my diet than most carnivores do.

I've seen it from both sides. Most meat-eaters I know eat the same five or six things over and over again. I know that's how it was for me when I ate meat. But once I gave up animal products, I was forced to try dozens of foods that I either used to ignore or that I didn't even know existed in the first place. And a lot of those "weird" things are now my favorite foods.

When I was a kid, we ate American cuisine—pizzas, burgers, chili, chicken, and so on. Once in a while at my grandma and grandpa's place, we'd order Chinese food from our local spot, The Golden Gate.

But we never had Indian food. We definitely wouldn't have been making a family outing to a place like Babani's, that Kurdish restaurant in Minneapolis where I used to wait tables.

If you take the typical American diet and just remove all the meat and dairy, sure, that might leave you with some limited and pretty depressing options.

But eating a plant-based diet doesn't have to be like that. Not even close.

But how do you get enough protein?

In my humble opinion, everyone needs to calm the fuck down about protein.

It's become such a big buzzword. Every other food advertisement on TV seems to be bragging about how much protein everything has.

It's easy to understand what people are thinking. They figure carbs equal getting fat, and sugar equals getting fat, and of course fat equals getting fat. So what does that leave? Protein. People think that if they just eat plain chicken breasts all day, they must be in the clear.

But that logic is flawed for two reasons: For one thing, you need to cover all the different categories of food in your diet. Carbohydrates are what fuel your brain function, for example. So when you starve yourself of carbs, you're starving your brain.

(And, by the way, I think fear of carbs is way overrated. Personally, I am always carb-ing it up. I don't give a shit. If carbs are supposed to make you fat, then, well…I'm still waiting.)

More importantly, when you eat more of any one thing than your body needs, your body turns the rest of it into fat. That applies just the same to grilled chicken breasts and anything else that's loaded with protein.

In reality, if you are anything like the average American, you are in zero danger of not getting enough protein. Most Americans eat about twice as much protein as they really need. It's not always easy to find unbiased sources of information on the internet, but hopefully we can all agree that WebMD isn't in PETA's pocket. And here's what they have to say:

"Most Americans get more than enough protein each day, maybe […] because of animal sources like meat, poultry, and eggs. Although important in the diet, extra protein will not help you build more muscle or make you stronger. When you're consuming too much of it, you're probably taking in more calories and fat than your body needs."

You're ideally supposed to get 10-35% of your calories from protein. Unless you're a bodybuilder or an athlete, that's only about 46 grams a day for women and 56 grams a day for men.

(And I would even question whether that's an inflated number, because there's a huge industry built around selling people protein powders and protein bars. I wouldn't be remotely surprised if that industry is influencing the conversation a little bit.)

To put things in perspective: The bread I eat has six grams of protein per slice. So I could have two pieces of toast and I'd have almost a quarter of a normal person's protein for the day. Just a handful of peanuts has seven grams of protein.

Although many people don't know it, almost every food you can think of contains protein. Sure, candy doesn't. But spinach has a higher ratio of protein as a percentage of calories than beef does. Hell, a bag of frozen peas can have 20 grams of protein.

So where do vegans get protein? From food, just like everyone else. Some of the best sources of protein are plant-based, such as lentils, beans, quinoa, soy-based foods like tofu and tempeh, and seitan, which is wheat-based.

If you're trying to build or repair muscle, some extra protein is great. But that really only applies to athletes and bodybuilders. If you're a normal person with a normal activity level, all you need is a balanced diet, and that can be achieved solely through plant-based foods.

I get all the nutrition I need without the "help" of any animal products. When I go get my blood levels checked out, everything's fine.

And I barely even take any vitamins. When you take vitamins in pill form, you don't really absorb a lot of those nutrients anyway. That's why your pee is so yellow. You're just pissing those vitamins right out. Vitamin pills don't work. You need get your vitamins from food.

In order to make veganism work, you need to make a plan to get all the nutrients you need. And you also have to understand exactly what you're eating.

That's an issue a lot of new vegans encounter. That's why you'll sometimes hear people say that they tried going vegan but it didn't "work." If you stop eating foods that were giving you certain nutrients, you're going to have to replace those nutrients somehow. You can't just start eating salads—at least, not the same salads you used to eat, only without the meat. If I eat a salad, it's got spinach and lentils and nuts and all the things my body needs for proper nourishment.

Obviously, there are still some people—even some pretty smart ones—who believe that an athlete who doesn't eat meat will never perform as well as they could have if they had just chowed down on a steak from time to time to get all of that great protein and zinc and iron and whatever else people still think you can only get from eating animals.

For those people, and for the record, here's a list of some high-profile athletes who have publicly identified themselves as vegan or vegetarian:

- Tony Gonzales – Arguably the greatest and most durable NFL tight end of all time.
- Arien Foster – Pro Bowl running back who led the NFL in rushing in 2010.
- Ricky Williams – Another Pro Bowl running back, and a man who once said, "I wouldn't eat a chicken if it dropped dead in front of me holding a sign that said 'Eat Me.'"
- Prince Fielder – 6-time MLB All-Star and 2007 National League Home Run Champ.
- Robert Parish – 9-time NBA All-Star and 4-time champion who played in the NBA for 21 years.
- Venus Williams – 22-time Grand Slam winner who switched to a raw vegan diet after being diagnosed with an autoimmune disease called Sjögren's syndrome.
- Georges Laraque – 14-year NHL veteran and a vegan since 2009.
- Carl Lewis – 10-time Olympic medalist.
- Dave Scott - The winningest Iron Man triathlete ever.
- Mac Danzig – A recently-retired UFC fighter and a vegan since 2004.

There may not be a ton of us yet. But that list alone shows you that elite athletes can indeed reach their peak potential without eating animals or animal products.

Personally, when athletes I know become vegan, I hear the same three things over and over again: They say they have more energy, they have better endurance, and they have quicker recovery times after workouts and games.

Getting complete and fully-balanced nutrition from plants can be done pretty easily. If you want more proof, well, take a look at the handsome guy on the cover of this book.

Fine. But isn't vegan food ridiculously expensive?

This one really gets me.

Yes. Sure. Eating a plant-based diet can be expensive. But it doesn't have to be. If you eat out all the time, you probably spend more money on food than I do.

More importantly, cancer treatment is expensive. And I believe that's what you get from eating shitty food—especially shitty animal-based food.

It's funny—I've noticed that a lot of the people who ask me this question live in very nice, very expensive houses. They drive expensive cars and wear designer clothes. But somehow, when it comes to food, all of a sudden they need to cut corners and eat the cheapest, easiest thing they can possibly get their hands on.

Here's a quote from the good people at the Meat Institute, the trade association run by and for the U.S. meat industry: "Americans spend less than any other developed nation in the world on food broadly and on meat and poultry specifically."

They're saying that like it's something we should be proud of. But to me, it just highlights one of the main problems with our food culture: We are raised to eat the cheapest food we can get, without asking any questions about how our food was raised, how it got to be so cheap, and what that cheap meat will cost us, health-wise, in the long run.

According to the Meat Institute, Americans spend 6.4% of disposable income on food. For comparison's sake, I wonder how much disposable income people spend on their cell phone bills. And in the scheme of things, what's more important?

I know people who live in $400,000 houses with a couple of $30,000 vehicles in the garage who are able to look at me with a straight face and tell me it's "too expensive" to eat healthy.

Really? When you're going to buy a car, no one ever says, "What is the absolute cheapest, easiest, most convenient car I could purchase?" And yet when it comes to food, people seem to ask, "What's on sale?" Everyone needs to have the biggest high-definition TV they can possibly fit in their living room, but they somehow can't stretch their budget to afford organic vegetables. Look, I like nice houses and nice things, too. But if my body doesn't feel as healthy as it can, then, to me, all those other things don't matter. I want to eat high quality food. To me, that's just as important as anything else I could spend my money on.

Of course, not everyone is wealthy. There are more bills to pay today than our parents had to deal with. People have student loan payments and interest on credit cards. In my own lifetime, car insurance didn't used to be mandatory, but now it is. Health insurance is basically mandatory now, too. I wouldn't say you have to have a cell phone, but most people are operating at a disadvantage without one. That's a luxury that's turned into a necessity. You don't have to have cable TV and the internet at your house, but pretty much everyone does.

And wages haven't gone up nearly enough to account for all the new expenses. It's tough enough making ends meet without spending more on food. I get it.

But at the same time, sometimes I think people's financial situations can't be quite as dire as they claim. Everybody's talking about how broke they are these days, but it seems like everybody gets a new phone every two or three years, even if their old one still works fine.

There's always a new videogame system everyone has to get. A few years back, everyone needed to get a big flat screen TV, and pretty soon everyone's probably going to decide that now they need one of those new curved TVs instead.

It seems like, no matter how tight money is, dudes always find a way to own a pair of Jordan's. Girls always have a bunch of pairs of shoes. There's always a line outside the Apple store when the new iPhone 17 comes out.

When I was young, it felt like everyone my family knew drove old used cars. But now, most people I know either lease or they trade in their old car every few years for the latest model.

I mean, I moved to L.A. recently, and in the first week I was here, I saw two different homeless guys who had cell phones.

All of these things are great. I own plenty of unnecessary stuff myself. But all of these things will become instantly meaningless if you go to the doctor tomorrow and the doctor says you have a fatal disease because of all the cheap unhealthy shit you've been eating all your life. If that day ever comes, we all know you would gladly turn in your car and your phone and all of your other stuff in exchange for a clean bill of health. So why not make your health a priority now, before it's too late?

In today's society, it seems like no one can afford the necessities, but somehow everyone finds money for some luxuries. People will drop serious coin for the clothes that go on the outside of their bodies, with little or no regard for what's going inside.

I'm sure it's partially because good food isn't a status symbol. Organic groceries don't get you chicks the same way nice cars do, do they? (Even though the Whole Foods where I live seems like a raging pick-up joint.)

My mom made a really good point one time. She believes one of the reasons people cut corners on food is because food isn't a fixed cost. This particularly applies to people on a tight budget. Most of the other big expenses aren't flexible. Your rent's a fixed cost. So is your car payment. Your utility bill and your phone bill might change from month to month, but no matter how high they get, you still have to pay them in full.

Food is the one place in the budget where people have some wiggle room. If you have a hundred bucks, you can spend a hundred bucks that week. But if you can only spend fifty, you can make that work, too. No one is holding you to any set cost, or to any set quality or quantity of food. So when it comes to food shopping, it's easy to see how price can become the primary consideration. That's the one area you can cut when everything else is bleeding you dry.

But I think that's a short-sighted way of looking at things. (And believe me: I say that as someone who has been broke myself.) If money is tight, it's even more important to eat healthy. If you have a poor diet, you're likely to get sick in the long run, and your healthcare costs will far outweigh what you could have been spending all along on more nutritious (and better tasting) food.

I don't think most people realize how much better they could feel on a day-to-day basis if they treated their body the way their body wants to be treated. Many people also don't realize that you don't necessarily have to spend more money on food in order to eat healthier. You just need to learn what foods give your body the nutrients it needs and which crap your body doesn't want, and then reprioritize your food purchases accordingly.

And by the way, not all "fixed" costs are created equal. Heat and hot water are legitimate fixed costs. Health insurance is a fixed cost. But ask yourself: Are all the rest of your "fixed costs" really as fixed as they seem? There's a bare minimum you need to spend to live in a decent place in a decent neighborhood, but how far above that minimum do you need to go in order to be happy? Do you need to drive the best car you can possibly squeeze out of your budget, or can you get by with something a little more modest?

I know how it sounds for me to suggest you should live in a smaller house or drive a different car just so you can eat healthy organic food. But it's all about priorities. If I don't feel as healthy as I possibly can, to me, all that other stuff doesn't mean shit.

What's more, if you're on a tight budget, there's a good chance eating vegan might actually be more affordable than the alternatives. Veganism actually gets pretty cheap once you start buying dry goods—beans, rice, lentils and so on—in bulk and cooking for yourself. Not only are a lot of dry vegan goods inexpensive, unlike meat, they never spoil, so the money you spend on groceries doesn't just end up in the garbage.

You can freeze vegetables, too, and it doesn't compromise their nutritional content. I buy big bags of frozen spinach and frozen kale for my smoothies, and since they're frozen, I never have to throw any of that food away, either.

There's a popular book called *Eat Vegan on Four Dollars a Day*. Personally I've never read it, but, based on my experience, I'm sure that could be done pretty easily.

On the other hand, can you imagine trying to eat non-vegan on that tight of a budget? Even if you buy the cheapest, sketchiest ground beef, that's going to be tough to pull off. Even if you just got some generic Chef Boyardee-type stuff from the 99 Cents Store, you're still only getting four cans a day, and that sounds like some pretty sad mealtimes right there.

It sounds really difficult for a busy person to maintain this lifestyle—especially someone who's on the road a lot.

Preparation is the key. But that goes for anyone who wants to eat right, whether they follow a plant-based diet or not.

When you're away from home, your options are limited, and you tend to eat at strange hours, especially in my line of work. Whether you're vegan or not, you have two choices: Plan ahead, or wind up eating shitty fast food. And guess what? If you're old enough to read this book, it might be time to outgrow Mickey D's.

Okay. So, wait, no meat at all? Don't you miss bacon?

Nope. Not at all.

It's funny—people always tell me about how much they love the taste of meat and how they could never give it up. But if that's the case, then why doesn't anyone just boil meat in water and eat it plain? Maybe it's because you don't like meat as much as you think you do. I bet you like the taste of salt and seasonings and the sauces just as much as the meat itself, if not more.

You might say you love chicken nuggets. But how good are they without the barbecue sauce, or the sweet and sour, or the Buffalo sauce? How exciting is a burger without catsup and mustard and lettuce and tomato and pickles and onions on there? Is it really the meat you like? Or is it the whole flavor profile?

You can find meat substitutes that taste and resemble your nuggets or your burgers closely enough that, when you add all the other non-meat elements you also crave, all of a sudden, it doesn't feel like you're making this huge, drastic change.

I believe people often feel compelled to keep eating meat for reasons that go beyond flavor. Nostalgia and tradition are also really powerful forces. Why does everyone love bacon so much? Partially because it tastes good. Sure. But it's also because everybody remembers waking up to that smell when they were a kid and then having breakfast with their family.

It's a strong emotional bond. But once you break that spell, you might realize you weren't quite as attached to meat as you thought you were.

Again, it's all about what you choose to make important in your life. Most of us were raised to think about food the same way. Eat what's cheap and what tastes good and what's easy. Murder pigs and cows and eat them, but let dogs and cats sleep in our beds. Some birds are pets, but other ones are dinner.

If you want to change the way you eat, that thought process needs to change. For me, taste and smell still enter the equation.

They just aren't the sole factors that go into my decisions about what I eat.

When you start making positive changes in your diet, you start taking pride in looking and feeling physically fit. If you have an active lifestyle, you notice that eating better food improves your performance.

And when you take pride in eating things that are good for you, you acquire a taste for foods in a whole new way, because you associate those tastes with all the positive benefits. Are green drinks with a bunch of kale and other dark green veggies as tasty as chocolate milkshakes? Not really. But like tons of other people, I've come to love the way they taste, because I know all the good things they do for my health and how good they make me feel.

When people hear someone like me start talking about plant-based diets, I understand their reaction. Even if they agree in theory, they tend to think, "Sure. But I could never do that." And you know what? If that's what you're thinking right now, you're probably right. If you try to change your entire diet overnight, chances are it will blow up in your face.

If you're considering moving in the direction of a meat-free or fully plant-based diet, let me pass along a few pieces of practical advice.

My first tip would be to start small. I would never recommend anyone try to make the change all at once. Most people can't just flip a switch and become a vegan. It doesn't work like that. Chances are, by day two or day three, you'll throw in the towel.

You can't just decide to give up everything you've been eating your entire life cold turkey. It's not any different than when people go on extreme exotic weight-loss plans. Inevitably, they hit the wall and give up.

This applies to any radical dietary change. I bet that if you went to Iceland or Japan or Zimbabwe and tried to adopt the local cuisine full bore, you'd want to give up after a couple of days. That doesn't mean the food in other countries is bad. Obviously, the locals love it. It just means that they're used to it and you're not.

But if you hung in there, eventually that food would taste perfectly normal to you. Believe it or not, if you came back to the States after a few years, you might even find that you've lost your taste for a couple things you grew up with. That's the way our brains and our taste buds work.

If you're accustomed to eating meat, it's a big change to switch to a 100% plant-based diet. Because most people essentially eat a 0% plant-based diet. They might snack on some fruit or some nuts here or there, but otherwise, every single meal they eat every day contains at least one animal product, even if you sometimes forget—or don't know—that stuff is in there. You can't just shut that habit off like a water faucet.

But it's in your best interests to try. Even if some of the animal products you consume aren't all that bad for you, incrementally they will mess your systems up and challenge your ability to stay healthy. If you're eating animal products every time you eat, like most people are, then you're never giving your body a break. It's a constant bombardment.

So ease into it. Take baby steps. Start with one meal per week. Don't even worry about making that meal strictly vegan. Just start with something vegetarian.

Maybe you usually get burgers from Burger King once a week. Well, next week, instead of grabbing those fast food burgers, why not buy some veggie burgers and grill those up instead? You might find out that they're not too bad. You'll also probably notice that they're a little bit cheaper than fast food. And later on that night, you might notice that you don't have that indigestion you get from fast food. You might feel pretty good actually.

Then start to build from there. The next time you go to the store, instead of buying regular milk, pick up some almond milk instead. See if you like that. And then continue on, one small change at a time.

I find that as people get comfortable with some plant-based food alternatives, and as they become more informed about the positive changes they've started making in their diets, the process starts to snowball.

Maybe their doctor has been telling them to cut back on bacon. So they try Smart Bacon instead. It might not taste exactly the same, but when they realize the difference in nutritional content, they say, "Hey, I could get used to this." Or maybe they try a plant-based mayo and realize they like it even better than the old stuff. (Admit it: Mayo is kind of gross.)

As you become familiar with a wider range of vegetarian foods, the next stage might be to pick one day to go fully vegetarian. Pick three meals and maybe a couple of snacks that don't contain any meat.

If that goes okay, consider making that an ongoing weekly thing. Call it a Meatless Monday. And then if you decide you're ready to take it a step further, why not cut out the eggs and the dairy and make it a full-on Vegan Monday?

Integrate the changes slowly. As you go along, you might just find that eating bacon cheeseburgers somehow doesn't seem quite as important as it used to.

If you're used to a traditional meat-eating diet, you may find going vegetarian more do-able than fully eliminating all animal products. And it's easy to see why. Vegetarianism is a way easier transition. If you go to Starbucks, they sell an egg white, spinach, and feta wrap. Even if you don't eat meat, you can still order that. It gets harder once you stop eating eggs or dairy. Starbucks has nothing to offer you. And neither do a lot of other places.

I have nothing against vegetarians. I was one for ten years. I can understand the mentality. You feel like at least you're not hurting animals, which is obviously a good thing.

The bad news is that the dairy industry is pretty awful, too. You're not killing cows. But you are still paying someone to torture them. And that's not a whole lot better. The same goes for most of those chickens that are laying the eggs you eat.

Plus, everybody knows cheese isn't good for you. It's basically pure cholesterol. In terms of saturated fat, it's right up there with burgers.

But that's just how I see it. Obviously, I feel very strongly about not eating animals or animal products. However, let me stress again that eating plant-based food doesn't have to be an all-or-nothing decision. Everyone is going to decide for themselves how much they're willing or able to change. Maybe you'll switch from chicken nuggets to veggie nuggets, and that's it. That's fine. That's more than fine. That's great.

There's a whole spectrum of diets to choose from, and I am willing to accept and respect people on all points along that spectrum, as long as they're making informed choices. Every little bit matters. If you only changed 10% of your diet, that would still be meaningful, both for you and for the world around you.

On the other hand, if you believe you're ready to take the plunge into a fully plant-based existence, let me pass along some of the wisdom of my experience. I promise: It's not as hard as the naysayers like to pretend it is.

I don't think it's as uncommon as it used to be, either. I don't know what the statistics say, but it does seem like veganism is talked about more and more in the mainstream. I don't think I'm as much of an outsider as I used to be.

I even saw that Beyoncé did the 22-Day Vegan Challenge. Afterwards, all she could talk about was how much weight she lost and how great she looked. Personally, I would have preferred if she focused more on the health benefits than on how radiant it made her skin. But if Beyoncé thinks trying veganism for a couple weeks is a trendy thing to do, then that shows how far plant-based diets have come.

If you don't employ a full-time personal chef like Beyoncé

does, there are several challenges you'll need to prepare yourself for when it comes to gathering vegan food on a daily basis.

As I've said, switching to a plant-based diet doesn't need to cost a lot of money. People love to exaggerate about that, almost as much as they like saying that soy milk gives men tits. (Another thing about that, by the way: Soy is a basic component of a lot of Asian cuisines. If soy gave dudes man-boobs, then wouldn't every guy in Japan have cleavage?) But make no mistake—a plant-based diet can definitely be pricey if you don't have a game plan.

And bear in mind that switching to a plant-based diet doesn't automatically mean becoming healthy. If I wanted to, I could live on Oreos and almond milk and pasta and Twizzlers. Those are all 100% vegan. But I don't think that diet is an ideal recipe for long-term health and happiness.

So let's assume you're thinking of adopting a plant-based diet in part because you want to become healthier and feel better. Let's talk about how you would do that.

When it comes to buying groceries, now you're really going to have to get in the habit of checking the ingredients in all the foods you buy. Chances are you have no idea what's hiding in some of those boxes.

For example, did you know Kellogg's Raisin Bran is not vegan? The vitamin D they add is animal-based. On the other hand, you might be surprised to learn that several major store brands of bacon bits contain no animal products whatsoever. It just goes to show—you can't judge a book by its cover, and you can't tell all that much about a product until you flip it over and read the label.

If you're on a budget, you might have to reevaluate your priorities a bit. Above all, you need to focus your spending on the basic staples which will give you the most nutritional bang for your buck. I happen to like pickles. But organic pickles can get pretty expensive, and they don't provide much in the way of calories or nutrition. So if money is an issue, well, you might to have to wait until those pickles—or whatever your thing might be—are on sale and stock up then.

I find that if you eliminate a couple of unnecessary or luxury items, you can usually come up with the extra few bucks to buy better quality organic produce. If you drink soda or buy junk food, that would be a really obvious place to cut back.

I used to really like orange juice. But when I first got serious about food, I came to realize that orange juice is basically just a bunch of sugar. And the organic stuff can get really expensive, especially during certain times of the year.

I also realized that if I didn't spend five or six bucks on juice, I could easily cover the extra 50 cents a pound for the organic fruits and veggies I was buying. So I stopped buying O.J., at least all the time.

It's really not hard. You just have to do a bit of prioritizing and a little bit of math.

Focusing on the amount of nutritional value you get for your dollar will change the way you look at food forever. For example, a box of normal kids' cereal costs about $4 and provides very little in the way of nutritional value. But for half that price, you can buy a box of oatmeal that will provide ten times the nutrition.

In an ideal world, you'd want to buy all organic fruits and vegetables. But in reality, you might find that buying all organic just isn't feasible. If you can't afford to eat everything organic, then you have to pick your poisons. And unfortunately, under our current food system, I do mean that literally.

But there's help available to you. Every year, an organization called The Environmental Working Group issues a list called the Dirty Dozen. The Dirty Dozen are the 12 most contaminated fruits and vegetables that it's most important to eat organic at any given time. The list changes every year, as farming practices evolve and as new pesticides and other evil shit get introduced.

(Fun fact: Did you know that run-of-the-mill non-organic store-bought cucumbers currently contain over 35 different pesticides?)

Staying on top of that list every year is a good start. Here's another helpful rule of thumb: If you have to choose, it is most important to buy organic with any food where you eat the skin, like apples or spinach. The surfaces of fruits and vegetables are the parts that get most exposed to pesticides back on the farm. So if necessary, go non-organic on avocados, bananas, oranges, and other foods where the peel gets thrown away.

Again, assuming that money is an issue, you'll probably need to familiarize yourself with more than one grocery store. I find buying locally-sourced organic stuff from a large grocery store chain tends to be more expensive, because, in those stores, organic foods are specialty items. In my local so-called "health food" store, I can usually find that same stuff cheaper. That's what the store specializes in, so they can often buy in bulk and negotiate better deals for themselves.

Weirdly enough, you can often find really random high-quality organic foods at places like Big Lots. Even stores like Marshall's and T.J. Maxx will sometimes carry really good, really healthy snack foods and protein bars that would cost twice as much at a grocery store.

Don't ask me why. These are the things you begin to learn when you stop eating what the system tells you to eat and instead you do some homework, do some exploring, and start figuring things out for yourself.

If you decide to embrace a fully plant-based diet, at some point you're going to have to eat a meal away from your house. Obviously, our world is not designed to cater to vegans. That means you're going to need a plan.

Finding vegan options at restaurants doesn't tend to be all that difficult anymore. But finding vegan sources of protein is a whole different story. That's why I always make sure I carry some good protein sources with me. I've always got a few protein bars in my bag. I always make sure I've got a bag of almonds with me, too, so no matter where I go, I know I have a good snack that's got a little protein and fat in it.

I also keep my bags of pre-cooked black lentils with me at all times. The ones I buy have over 40 grams of protein per bag, so I can just add those to a salad and I'm all set. As long as I've got those handy, I can eat in any restaurant in the world.

I always make sure I have some plant-based protein powders, too. I might find myself in some greasy spoon diner, and maybe the only thing on the menu that appeals to me is some sweet potato fries. But if I have my protein powder with me, I can make a little shake on the side, and, along with the fries, I've got my protein and my carbohydrates covered.

Sometimes you're going to have to get creative. Once, while I was wrestling over in Japan, I developed a hankering for some pasta. I managed to find some dry noodles and some sauce at a little international grocery store. And then I took that stuff back to my hotel and boiled it all up in a little teapot they provided in the room.

Mind you, this hotel room was miniscule. It was pretty much just me and a bed and this teapot with my dinner in it. There I was, all by my lonesome, boiling my pasta and then fishing it out. It wasn't pretty. But it got the job done.

Another time I ran into a little trouble trying to smuggle some vegan chili on a plane. I had the chili packed inside my carry-on in a microwaveable tub, and the tub got flagged. The TSA lady started in with the whole "no gels or liquids" spiel.

But I was ready for her.

"I'm diabetic," I said. "And I've got some food allergies, too." Once I said that, she waved me right through.

I've found that when you tell people you need things for medical reasons, that shuts down any type of judgment or bullshit questions. You can pretty much get away with anything.

I always travel with food. Wherever I go, I always bring a meal or two with me, so that when I hit the ground in a strange place, I know I'm covered for a while, until I get my local bearings. Then once I get to town, I'll hit up a Whole Foods or something like that and buy a couple of pre-made veggie sandwiches.

I also always travel with a cooler. I might drop thirty bucks at a Whole Foods to stock myself up for a weekend. That might sound like a lot to spend for a couple days' worth of food. But if you think about it, you could easily drop that much for one meal (of horrible food) at TGI Friday's, once you figure in a tip and maybe a drink or an appetizer.

One of the nice things about traveling with vegan food is that you don't have to worry nearly as much about it going bad. If I'm on a plane for a while, or if it's a minute before I get my food from Whole Foods into my cooler or into the fridge at the hotel room, I don't freak out. It's not like I've got a ham sandwich or something else that might give me food poisoning.

I always make sure I have a fridge in my hotel room. If there isn't one already in the room when I get there, the front desk always tries to charge me to bring it up. But once I tell them I need the fridge to keep some medicine cold, then miraculously it's always comped.

These are just some of the tricks of the trade. Staying plant-powered isn't always easy. And sometimes you've got to get creative. But once you get in the habit, I promise you, it's doable.

Although finding the kind of food I want to eat can be a challenge from time to time, in general there's never been a better time to be plant-based. There are so many great resources on the internet nowadays, especially for someone who travels as much as I do.

I recommend a website called HappyCow.net. (They also have an app.) Wherever you are, you can just type in a zip code and it tells you all the local restaurants that have vegan and vegetarian options, plus all the local health food stores.

If you're a vegetarian or a vegan, HappyCow might tip you off to some places in your town that you never knew existed. Even if you eat meat, give it a go next time you're bored and looking to try something different. Just see what comes up. You might find there's some spot you've driven past a thousand times that looks kind of interesting. Why not go check it out? What do you have to lose? I promise you, those greasy double cheeseburgers aren't going anywhere.

Vegan food has really come a long way, even just in the time that I've been eating it. At some of the vegan restaurants I go to, the food is so good it's easy to forget that you're not eating any animal products. There's one spot I love in Orlando called Ethos Vegan Kitchen. They have every type of comfort food you can imagine—calzones, pizza, sausage rolls, mac and cheese—you name it. I'm not saying everything on the menu is necessarily healthy for you. I'm sure the sodium is through the roof. But it's all vegan. And it's awesome.

Things are getting better everywhere. Even back in Milwaukee, the home of cheese and beer and brats, there are more and more places popping up which cater to vegans, or at least include some menu options with vegans in mind.

Back at Winona State, I used to hang out at a nightclub called Fitzgerald's. (Man, I could tell you some stories about Fitzgerald's. But that's a whole other book.) Fitzgerald's is closed down now. And in its place, they opened a natural foods co-op that's doing really well. There are also some newer cafes in town that serve hummus and pita sandwiches and stuff like that.

I'm sure the local Hardee's and Domino's are in no danger of going under anytime soon. But at least now you can see that people are opening their minds. There's demand for better, healthier options. It goes to show you how much of a shift is already underway.

That having been said, there is still a level of ignorance among some people. Back during my Ring of Honor days in Phil-

168

adelphia, I used to have an ongoing argument with the counter people at Taco Bell. I would order the Baja Chalupa. For those who may not be familiar, a chalupa is like a taco, only the shell is thicker, almost like fried waffle pizza crust bread. I used to dig it.

Anyway, Taco Bell didn't offer a bean and rice chalupa, so I would order the beef one and then tell them to make it with rice instead.

Every single time, they would charge me 50 cents extra for the rice. And every single time, I would try to explain that I wasn't getting extra rice. I was getting rice instead of meat. I didn't mind paying the same price, but why was I paying extra? We all know Taco Bell uses piss-poor meat, but were they really saying that their rice costs more than their beef?

I went as far as calling corporate Taco Bell. (Yeah, I know it was only 50 cents. It was the principle, dammit.) And corporate Taco Bell backed their counter people. They told me there was an extra charge because what I wanted was considered a special order.

Their cash registers literally had no way of substituting a vegetarian option for the meat option. The counter people could only ring in the rice as an extra. Their system was just not designed to accommodate vegetarians. I think I might well have been the first person who ever called them to complain about that.

A similar sort of incident occurred in England. I had an extended phone conversation with a pizza place, trying to explain that I wanted to order a pizza with no cheese.

At first, they thought I just wanted them to go easy on the cheese. After a good 30 minutes, I convinced them that if I ate cheese, I would die. (The way I figure it, I'm going to die someday, whether or not I eat cheese. So technically, that isn't a lie.)

When the guy finally showed up, he delivered me a box containing a plain pizza crust.

In my experience, there are some places in the world where veganism and vegetarianism aren't totally foreign concepts. Several years back, when I was over in Japan working for Dragon

Gate, I learned how to order a meatless Big Mac in Japanese. This was when I was still a vegetarian, so I wasn't worried about the cheese, or the special sauce, or whatever the hell might be lurking in their buns.

There were a bunch of us guys on a tour bus, and lots of times, at a rest stop in the middle of the night, the only place that would be open was a McDonald's.

I would just say, "Big Mac, no *niku*." *Niku* means meat.

The counter people didn't blink. They just made me a Big Mac with slices of tomato in place of the beef patties.

I tried the same thing in America. Once they figured out what the hell I was talking about, just like Taco Bell, they charged me 25 cents for eating tomato slices instead of those "two all-beef patties." And then the counter guy had to walk to the back and personally explain my order to the person who was going to assemble it.

That's right. It was easier to get a meatless McDonald's sandwich in a country where I don't speak the language than it was in the country where I was born and raised.

There are plenty of cultures where meat is viewed differently than it is in America. In those places, it's widely understood that some people don't eat animals. It's no big deal. But in my experience, Americans are very insulated. Some people have a hard time understanding that not everyone looks at food the same way as they do.

During that same tour in Japan, while I was enjoying my meatless Big Macs, one night a wrestler named El Generico (you may know him as Sami Zayn) ordered himself a burger. But one of the other wrestlers (who I will not name) decided to play a little prank, or a rib, as it's known in the wrestling business. This particular rib, coincidentally, involved a McRib.

Sami is a Muslim. He doesn't eat pork. But one of the wrestlers ordered Sami a McRib with no sauce and told him it was a burger. Sami started eating it, and then the guy started laughing his ass off.

Trust me; he was the only one laughing. Generico didn't find that joke very funny. He's a pretty laidback cat, so he just rolled with it. But you could tell it bummed him out. That's not funny, messing with someone's beliefs like that.

I started thinking about how I would have felt if that same guy had tried to slip me a burger. My stance on eating meat has nothing to do with religion, but eating meat still goes against my personal belief system.

To me, there's something kind of sacred about what you allow into your body. Tricking me into violating my beliefs crosses a pretty big line. But I also know that some people just don't understand that.

It's funny, no one would ever think of pulling that rib if a guy had a food allergy. Imagine if there was a guy with a peanut allergy, and you swapped out his almond butter with some Skippy. "Guys, get over here! Check it out—his throat's closing up! AHAHAHA!"

If you decide to become plant-based, unfortunately, you have to expect some occasional insensitivity, both from people you know and from strangers you come across. People don't seem to mind so much if you don't want to eat meat. But in my experience, oftentimes they don't want to hear about it.

If I post a picture of vegan food online, there are always one or two people who feel the need to lash out, or at least make some smartass comment. The way I look at it, in everyday life, we're bombarded by a constant stream of messages telling us to eat animals and eat animal products. It's everywhere you turn—television commercials, radio, billboards, and so on. So why get angry when one dude occasionally sticks up for eating plants? The meat industry is not suffering for publicity. Is it really so offensive to hear an alternative point of view?

Depending on where you live, when you go to a mainstream-style restaurant, you might see a wide variety of reactions from food servers when you try to explain that you don't eat animal products. When I'm in Los Angeles, it's not an issue. When I'm in Austin, Texas, it's pretty easy, too. But when I'm somewhere else in Texas…it can be a slightly different story. (Although even the Lone Star State—barbecue central—has come a long way.)

When I inform servers that I don't eat animals, for some reason some of them feel the need to tell me why they could never give up meat. Obviously, the topic strikes an emotional chord in them, so they feel compelled to offer a little rebuttal to my lifestyle.

I consider that a bit rude. I don't think it's a server's place to comment on someone else's diet. I was a waiter myself at one point in my life, so I think I understand the protocol and the job.

Would you like me to turn that around and tell you all the reasons why you shouldn't be eating what you do? I mean, if you ask me, it's even weirder that you eat animals, and that there's a massive industry that's based on stealing milk from mother cows and feeding it to people. But I'm not going to throw that in anybody's face, unless they ask me about it (or they buy my book).

I don't need the commentary. It's unnecessary and it's unprofessional. It's not your job to judge me because of what I eat. Your job is to serve me food, not to initiate a dialogue on our dietary lifestyles.

I've had the long drawn-out conversation about why I don't eat meat and dairy so many times that by now I've gotten pretty bored of it. So sometimes, to avoid it, I just tell my waiter or waitress that I'm allergic to all forms of animal products. That one works like a charm.

It's just like bringing food through airport security or getting a fridge in my hotel room. Once a server thinks I could die (and maybe sue them or the restaurant), the conversation seems to end there.

It's funny. When I'm a vegan, servers tell me they're "pretty sure" the garden salad doesn't contain any animal products. But when they think I'm allergic, well, that's when they tend to make the trip back to the kitchen to confirm it.

And in a roundabout way, I believe it's true. I believe that eating animal products over an extended period of time will increase my chances of developing cancer or other illnesses. Sure, maybe I won't break out in hives on the spot. But in ten or twenty years, those animal products might indeed kill me. That might not mean I'm allergic in the traditional sense, but if you take a long-term view of it, I'm not completely lying, either.

No matter how careful you try to be at restaurants, mistakes will inevitably happen. You order a salad and you tell your server you don't want any animal products. So they lose the chicken and the cheese, but then it comes out and you take a bite and you realize they forgot that the bacon bits they serve are meat. But you can't un-chew that first bite, or un-taste it.

A few years back, I was eating at an Asian restaurant in Minnesota with a friend of mine. She's a vegetarian, so we decided to share some "mock duck."

The food came out, and we were both blown away by how good it was. The texture was spot-on. This was some of the best mock meat we'd ever eaten. But then, as you've probably guessed, we got the bill, and it turned out the food we'd been enjoying was not mock duck, but some very real orange chicken.

The waiter knew he had screwed up. He suggested that maybe we could just pay for the egg rolls we ate.

I suggested that maybe we would pay for nothing. The conversation got a bit animated and things escalated a little bit. But it only went so far, since the guy couldn't really speak English. And by that point, the damage had been done.

That led to a rough night. When you abstain from meat for a long time and then you eat it again, it can create a memorably uncomfortable digestion process. Unless you've been through that yourself, I guess maybe it's hard to relate. But take my word for it. That sucked.

Sooner or later, something like that is probably bound to

happen. It comes with the territory.

Non-vegans will sometimes act like incidents like that aren't a big deal. It comes down to a lack of knowledge, or maybe just a lack of awareness.

Back when I still ate cheese, someone might offer me some pepperoni pizza and then tell me to just take off the pepperoni. But guess what? That doesn't make it any better.

Think of something that really repulses you. What if there was cat sausage on that pizza, for example? If someone pulled the little slabs of cat off, would you be cool with eating that pizza? The flavor would still be there. The grease would still be there. And even if you couldn't tell the cat meat had been there, you would know it was. There's no way in hell you would touch that slice.

I should have just told the waiter in the Chinese restaurant I was allergic to chicken. That probably would have solved everything.

I know some people might wonder: If my friend and I enjoyed the orange chicken that much, well, then, why don't we just eat chicken sometimes? It's an understandable question, to an extent. But to me, it misses the point.

Sure, sometimes meat or cheese still look and smell good to me. If I were to take a bite, they would probably taste good, too—although I'm not entirely sure of that, because your palate does change.

But that's not what it's about. When it comes to food, my priorities don't begin and end with taste and smell. A lot of thought went into my decision to not eat animal products. I did not arrive at my beliefs lightly. And because I have my reasons, meat and dairy are literally no longer appetizing to me.

If I decided to scarf down a slice of pizza one day, my body probably wouldn't feel too good afterwards. But even worse, I'd feel disappointed in myself for choosing a couple fleeting minutes of taste over my long-term principles. And when you look at it that way, sticking to a plant-based diet isn't that hard at all. It just comes down to what's important to you.

One last time, I want to be clear: The objective of this book isn't to try and convert people to veganism. It's about asking people to take a closer look at their food choices and the impact those choices have, both on their health and on the world at large.

My food journey, much like my career path, has led me to what some people would consider an unconventional and extreme lifestyle.

Every time I eat a meal, I consume zero animal products. That puts me all the way at one end of the dietary spectrum.

But we live in a society that programs us to accept that constant meat and dairy consumption is "normal." I sometimes ask people to tell me the last time they had a meal that didn't contain some form of meat, dairy, egg, or other animal product. Then I watch their blank stares as they realize they can't remember.

I hope by now you can see why that end of the spectrum is also extreme

I'm not saying my completely plant-based end of the spectrum is the absolute truth or the 100% "right" path to follow. But I am convinced that the other end of the spectrum—the animal-based diet we've all been sold—is absolutely misguided and extremely dangerous.

Hopefully, this book inspires you to see food in a whole new light, and offers some food for thought on the path to becoming a new and greater you.